A **YEAR** of
Intentional Parenting

*52 weekly vignettes gleaned from our work guiding
parents in finding their right way to parent*

Julie Freedman-Smith
and Gail Bell

 **FriesenPress**

Suite 300 – 990 Fort Street
Victoria, BC, Canada V8V 3K2
www.friesenpress.com

Edited by Virginia Durksen, Visible Ink Incorporated
Photography by Kenton Smith Photography

ISBN
978-1-4602-5103-4 (Hardcover)
978-1-4602-5104-1 (Paperback)
978-1-4602-5105-8 (eBook)

1. Family & Relationships, Child Care

Distributed to the trade by The Ingram Book Company

Table of Contents

Parenting Power™ is the trademark for our approach to working with parents. When we refer to Parenting Power throughout this book, the trademark is implicit in our use of the business name.

Julie and Gail
www.parentingpower.ca
admin@parentingpower.ca
www.facebook.com/parentingpower
Twitter: @parentingpower

Message from the authors

We met while working together in a school in Calgary, Alberta, Canada. At that time, we saw many loving families who wanted to set their kids up for success but weren't quite sure how to do it. Together, we hoped to make a difference in the lives of those parents and, correspondingly, those children.

We started our company in 2002 and called it Parenting Power™. We loved the definition of power as *the ability to effect change*. We believed then, and still do, that when parents take responsibility for their own behaviour, they can effect change in the behaviours of their children. Consequently, the children learn to take responsibility and the whole family is working together to effect great change in their community and the world at large.

As our own families grew, and we continued to work with our clients, we held on to our belief that there is more than one right way to parent. Each individual brings different experiences, values and dreams to a family. Each child is unique; what one child needs will be different from what another needs.

When we taught children, we met students at their level and helped them grow and learn, setting them up for success every step of the way. We apply this same technique when working with families. We encourage you to see your family where it is right now, determine your values and the vision you have for your children as they grow. Then, have the courage to take the first step to get there. It doesn't have to be perfect; we will all make mistakes and we can learn from them.

The format of this book takes you through the year with 52 short articles. You may choose to read it chronologically, focusing on one piece per week. Perhaps you will randomly open the book to a page and start reading. Do what makes sense to you. We've built the book so that it can carry you through a year and then start again – our kids are always changing and what you need to read today may be quite different from what you need in the future.

We hope that this book makes a difference in your parenting life. Please drop us a note and let us know what you think.

Julie and Gail
www.parentingpower.ca
admin@parentingpower.ca
www.facebook.com/parentingpower
Twitter: @parentingpower

Parenting on purpose

What is parenting? For many, the first time we played the role of parent was while playing house at four years old. When we first find out that we are going to actually be parents, we throw ourselves whole-heartedly into the role: reading books, editing the scripts that our parents followed, asking questions, buying the props, doing everything we are supposed to do to fit that role.

When our children come along, there are so many amazing things to witness and experience. There are things that zap the life out of us too. So it is sometimes easier to just keep playing the role as it unfolds: naps, diapers, nursing, solid food, music class, gym class, preschool, parties, sports, lessons, homework!

Parents' lives can be so full of stuff to do that we don't leave time for the essential parts of parenting. The big problem here is that the extra jobs of parenting are about external things; they are not what is necessary for building the internal core of a self-disciplined, confident child.

This is what motivated us to focus on a year of *intentional* parenting.

> ### *Things parents do that are NOT parenting essentials*
>
> - Driving
> - Coaching
> - Scheduling extra-curricular activities
> - Friday movie night
> - Taking kids on trips
> - Shopping: buying the right outfits, sporting equipment
> - Finding the right piano teacher, personal trainer
> - Over-praising kids: bragging, tweeting and posting about them on Facebook and bumper stickers
> - Rescuing kids from their consequences
> - Paying for the best school
> - Financial support into adulthood

We know that all these extras seem like real parenting. In reality they are just part of the role. What is critical is when we leave the core of parenting out of the mix to make time for these external things.

Intentional parenting is the process of promoting and supporting the physical, emotional, social and intellectual development of a child from infancy to adulthood. Sounds easy right? NOPE!

The goal of this book is not to add a whole bunch of work to an already full plate. What we are actually saying is CHOOSE WHAT'S ON YOUR PLATE. Focus your attention and effort on the essentials of parenting.

THE ESSENTIALS OF PARENTING

This is where actual parenting requires our time and energy. Knowing that these are the essential parts of parenting helps us set our priorities as parents.

- Parenting is **presence** – eye to eye and shoulder to shoulder presence.

- Parenting is **discipline** – taking the time to set age-appropriate expectations, including morals and values, coupled with consequences.

- Parenting is **allowing your children to learn, grow and feel capable through their choices, both good and bad.** Our kids are going to make poor choices. That's where they learn the most.

- Parenting is about **providing opportunities to have purpose in the home through consistent responsibilities** – letting kids learn that they are capable and that they contribute to their community (family and beyond).

- Parenting is about **teaching values** to our kids through our daily behaviours while we are with them.

- Parenting is about **connection** – one-on-one connection.

- Parenting is **about making time to teach your children** to catch a ball and ride a bike and play a game. It is about teaching them that it is normal for people to disagree and then teaching them how to respectfully solve disagreements.

- Parenting is about **not** over-scheduling our kids. It is about **teaching them the schedules of life** – how long it takes to finish breakfast, brush teeth, get into coats and get into the car – not nagging and hounding them but letting them learn to manage it on their own.

This doesn't mean we won't be driving our kids or making meals. We are not going on strike. We are creating:

- Space in our thinking to determine what's important to us when it comes to the development of our kids

- Time in our calendars to allow that to happen

- Systems to allow it to happen – with respect to modelling what we want our kids to learn.

No mean feat! We've got a whole year in which to set out and learn from our mistakes. That's the way it works. We invite you to join us. The more, the merrier.

A **YEAR** of
Intentional Parenting

JANUARY

Ten things your kids need from you this year
A parent's job description

In a recent list of the year's most absurd reasons to call the emergency line, two really stood out:

> *Can an officer come over to tell my kids to go to bed?*
> *My son won't give me the remote control.*

There is no question that many parents feel like calling the police on their kids from time to time, but the fact that two people actually made these calls means that things are truly getting out of hand.

So let's get back to basics as we begin this year. We don't have to make a bunch of resolutions or earth-shattering changes as we get started. What we do need to remember and act on is as follows. If it seems like too much, just pick one for now.

- **Kids want parents to parent** – not to be their friends or to let them fly freely with no boundaries. They need us to set limits and to follow through.

- **Kids want to feel capable.** They can't if we won't let them. Please stop doing everything for your kids (stop solving their problems and helping them when they know how to do it themselves).

- **Kids need sleep.** You don't need a policeman to make this happen. You do need to make a bedtime plan (we'll help if you need us to) and then stick to it.

- **Kids need to know that you are the boss.** If your son won't give you the remote control, take the TV, unplug it and lock it in the trunk of your car if need be. Your son (or daughter) needs to know that technology is a privilege not a right.

- **Kids need responsibility.** Once they are contributing to the family community, they can have access to the privileges of technology, along with other great things a family provides.

- **Kids need to get out and exercise.** They also need access to healthy food. The very best way to teach them this is to model it. Kids learn what they live.

- **Kids need our time and our presence.** They need us to turn off the TV, put down our phones, close the lid on the tablet and be with them. They need to read books, play games, walk, cook and hang out WITH us. They need to look at us and know that we're looking back – not all the time, but definitely much of it.

- **Kids need us to advocate for them** – not to make excuses for them but to stand up and support them as they learn the lessons that they need to learn and make the changes that they need to make.

- **Kids need to learn from the consequences of their actions** – not to be rescued from them.

- **Kids need our love, hope and support.** They need us to believe in them because when we don't believe in them it is impossible for them to believe in themselves.

Make this the year that you step up and parent your kids responsibly. (Oh yeah, and teach them what a real emergency is so that they don't call 9-1-1 for the wrong reasons.)

Do your actions match your words?
Kids learn more from what we do than from what we say

Jana called us from Toronto in tears. *I just don't get it! When I tell my kids to do anything, they don't. I have to repeatedly call them to dinner, ask them to help and beg them to brush their teeth. Why won't they listen?*

Ontario, Chicago, Australia or England — it doesn't matter what language is being used. Many kids ignore one or both of their parents. Many of our clients complain of this same frustration. *It was different when we were kids. If my parents said do it, I did it right away. I would never have been able to say no.*

Was it really that way? It's hard to say for sure. Perhaps it is selective memory or perhaps our parents had other means of getting us to listen.

Each generation develops its own parenting strategies. When we were kids, we knew what would happen if we didn't listen. Views on discipline strategies have changed so drastically in the last two generations, many are struggling to figure out how to get their kids to cooperate. Awareness of the situation is the first step in finding a solution.

Let's look at what happens when Jana needs her kids to come to dinner. They are downstairs watching their favourite TV show, which is just about finished. She calls them from the kitchen. *Are you guys ready for dinner?* She doesn't get a reply so she heads to the top of the stairs. *Guys, are you ready for dinner?*

Kind of.

Wow – they heard her. But they aren't turning off the TV even though the show they were watching is done.

Jana heads downstairs. *It's dinner time guys. Are you coming?*

The kids are still watching the commercials for what's coming next. *I really want to watch just one more show mom, please can we watch it?*

WHAT PART OF IT'S TIME FOR DINNER DID YOU NOT UNDERSTAND?! Jana grabs the remote, turns off the TV and chases the kids up the stairs. Everyone sits at the table and eats in frustrated grumbles. *I don't like this. Why did you make this?*

One can only imagine the script for the rest of the meal until everyone calms down and the argument is forgotten. Except it won't be forgotten because in many families the same script replays itself each day.

Why won't Jana's kids listen? They *are* listening – to her actions. Her words and her actions are saying two different things. Let's review the scenario and watch what her actions are telling the children.

1. Jana calls from the kitchen. She asks a question but her actions tell them they can ignore her because she is far away and she won't make them listen the first time.

2. Jana calls from the top of the stairs. She asks a question again and doesn't react to their non-committal response. At this point she has given no direct instructions to her kids with her words. Her actions say, "Don't bother listening to me yet." And that's exactly the reaction she is getting from her kids.

3. Jana heads downstairs. She asks if they are coming and they answer her that they would rather not.

4. The fourth time is different. She yells a question at them this time. The yelling is one clear action – they know that they are supposed to listen when she yells. Other actions also show she means it. She turns off the TV and moves her kids upstairs.

Jana's words spoke four times, as did her actions. But it was only the actions she used in the fourth approach that finally showed her kids that she needed them to stop what they were doing and go upstairs for dinner.

With Jana aware of her actions, the next step was making a plan to change them. We asked Jana what she wanted the situation to look like. She wanted her kids to show respect by listening to her the first time. She felt that their actions were communicating disrespect. Actions speak loudly to all of us.

Jana wanted the kids to listen to her the first time she told them to come for dinner. We gave her a few real-life parenting tools.

1. **Be sure that your kids know your expectations and the consequences of their actions before the TV goes on.**

   - *When this show ends, it will be time for dinner. I will give you one warning and I expect you to turn off the TV and come upstairs as soon as you are asked. When you show me you can do this, you will get a chance to do it again tomorrow. When you show me you have trouble getting up from the TV, we'll skip TV tomorrow and then try again the next day.*

2. **Check in to be sure that the communication is clear.**

   - *What did you hear me say? What will happen if you don't come?*

3. **When it is time for the warning, go to the children so that you can be there to follow through immediately.**

You will only tell them one time before you make them act. Don't give them the chance to pretend that they didn't hear you.

4. **Say what you mean; don't ask questions.**

- *It is time to turn off the TV and come up for dinner. (Not, Are you guys ready for dinner?)*

5. **When they do what you asked, recognize the result.**

- *I knew you could do this!*

6. **When they don't do what you asked, explain the consequences.**

- *Looks like you need me to turn this off today. And tomorrow we won't turn the TV on, then we can try again the next day. I see you are upset, please head upstairs for dinner now.*

Frustrating parenting moments happen to everyone. Begin with awareness of your communication style. Align your words and actions. Be respectful to everyone in your family by using one of our favourite mantras: ACT don't YAK!

Organization
Routines to build with your kids

The other day was a perfect example: Due to the cold weather, one of us got up to go running but decided against it. That left a whole hour to do things that needed to get done. But, that hour stretched a bit – getting to the shower and breakfast took longer than usual. All of a sudden it was time to take the kids to school and things weren't ready. The mistake – a change in routine.

You probably have your morning routine planned out – you know when you are getting into and out of the shower so that it coordinates with your spouse's shower and your kids' toilet flushes. Some people have everything planned out down to having the breakfast bowls on the table and the bags by the door or even in the car the night before. Planning is how parents make sure that they have what they need and get where they are going.

And yet, even though some things are organized, families often end up leaving their houses in a tizzy with half-open backpacks slung over shoulders, breakfast in hand, permission forms signed at a red light on the way to school. Why does this craziness persist?!

Having adult routines is a good start, but it is not the whole picture. We may have a plan for when we think breakfast should start/finish and when we need to be driving away. Our children, however, are not mind-readers and depending on them to be psychic can be a real let-down. Many of us think we are using routines but they are only effective if they are consistent and everyone knows what is expected of them. If we do not communicate our plans with our kids (and spouses), we cannot expect them to follow suit.

Routines can be used in the morning to get us out the door, but also throughout the day in those tricky, hassle-filled times. Some of our most valued routines are the Getting-Home-From-School routine or the Getting-Out-The-Door-To-Choir-Practice routine. One of our families is just building a Get-Ready-For-Hockey-And-Don't-Forget-Anything routine.

Chances are, if you have one or more areas of parenting that are really working for you, you have created a reliable routine that your children know inside and out. Maybe it's the bath or bedtime scenario. If it's working, take a look at why. The likelihood is that you have outlined for yourself the tasks that need to get done, who is doing them, the order in which they occur and you have clearly taught your children all of that information. It is most likely repeated daily with the odd "special occasion" exception – even then, you probably have an abbreviated routine that works in its place.

At Parenting Power we always encourage parents to take the time to teach children what you need them to do. They are not born knowing how to schedule their lives, but they are often ready to try and eager to please. This process can begin when our children are quite young.

Let's go back to that morning routine. If you have a plan for how you get organized, involve your children in developing a plan that will work for them. Spend some time deciding the sequence of the tasks. If you have a child that is starving in the morning but dawdles like crazy when getting dressed, put dressing before eating. The motivation of breakfast will move the first task along. In our experience, this may require an apron being worn by some children during breakfast – and it works!

Remember to discuss the timing of the tasks with your children and make sure that it is realistic. Just because you can guzzle a bowl of cereal in two minutes doesn't mean that your five-year-old can. Have some timing milestones noted as well – at the table by 7:35, brushing teeth by 7:55, boots on at 8:01. Then, help kids to know when those times are. Set an alarm for 7:50 to alert your family that there are five minutes left for breakfast. This stops you from nagging and helps kids to feel independent.

That really is the whole point of this exercise. By establishing routines with our children (and mapping them out with charts – pictures and words), we help our children to know what is expected. Life becomes more predictable and kids feel capable because they are doing things for themselves.

Work out the plan with your kids and do it with them for a few days – help them follow the chart. Then let them try it on their own and encourage their efforts. If most of the plan is working but some things are a disaster – rethink those parts. Working with our children is a lot easier than working against them.

Now, a warning! A little knowledge is a dangerous thing. Often parents receive this information and try to do too much too soon. They want to move directly from chaos to structure in two days, get overwhelmed and don't follow through. Please take our advice and pick one time of day and one routine and do it until it is the norm. You will move forward with baby steps. Home organizers will tell you to take 15 minutes a day to clean out one drawer at a time while de-cluttering your home. The same rule applies when de-cluttering your family chaos. You may be able to handle a bunch of new routines, but it is the little people in your life who really have to learn them.

Remember – add new routines gradually. Don't overwhelm your family. Focus on what your children are doing and trying to accomplish. Notice effort. Let them have input in as much of the routine as possible but make sure that there are targets for them to meet so that they clearly understand what is expected. Good luck!

Five Rs of parenting
Building blocks for parents

In an effort to protect children from the world at large, parents can fall into a pattern of puffing children up with false praise and grandiosity to build self-esteem. These techniques have been proven to backfire, resulting in children who feel tremendous pressure to live up to the false praise and who are devastated when they cannot.

At Parenting Power we believe that kids are capable and that one of the greatest gifts we can bring to our children daily as our lives (and theirs) pass us by is the awareness and understanding of the following five principles. Let us look briefly at each one to begin to understand them ourselves and how their wisdom will enhance the lives of our young people and the world as a whole.

REAL LIFE
When we first bring infants into the world, and as they grow, we have a tremendous inclination to protect them from the harder parts of life. We want each experience to be new and special. We want them to love themselves the way we love them.

Of course each child born into this world is unique. Each has strengths and weaknesses and deserves every opportunity. Each child is unique; therefore, being unique is normal. All children will experience both good and bad in each day. To this end, we need to be sure that we don't set them up to believe that they are *not* normal. Normal is a pretty great thing to be.

It also means that we need them to realise that bedtime, mealtime, toilet training, school and everything in between are parts of real life. As parents, we need to have a heightened awareness that we are not making excuses for our children to get out of doing what is expected. We have a responsibility to teach them about real life and they have a responsibility to meet the requirements of that life.

RESILIENCE

Resilience is the ability to withstand adversity and to carry on. It is something that many parents wish for their children. However, permitting children to learn this ability is not easy. Wouldn't it be wonderful if our children could become wise without suffering any hardships? In order for anyone to learn how to withstand a fall and carry on, he or she must first experience the fall.

The great news is that the very first falls our children experience are pretty tiny. Waiting until tomorrow to have that candy, or not making the team, can seem really hard for our children, but they can persevere and learn the beginnings of frustration tolerance. Belief in their own resilience will enable them to try, learn and grow from mistakes and failures that will occur many times in their lives. What's more, experiencing adversity and learning from it helps individuals to be more compassionate both inwardly and with others, eventually teaching our children relationship skills required in this interdependent world.

RESPONSIBILITY

Webster's New College Dictionary defines self-esteem as "an attitude of acceptance, approval and respect toward oneself, manifested by personal recognition of one's abilities and achievements and an acknowledgement and acceptance of one's limitations."

In her book *The Self-Esteem Trap*, Polly Young-Eisendrath observes that "good self-esteem comes from actual accomplishments and relationships. It is a by-product of doing some things well, accepting your limitations (when you need help from others) and seeing the good consequences of your own influence."

In the interest of time and ease, parents often have a tendency to do for their children tasks that the children can do for themselves. Increasing our awareness of these very tasks and teaching our children to undertake age-appropriate responsibilities is a critical part of parenting. When children learn new tasks, practise them and use discipline to perform them properly, they feel capable. Strengths and weaknesses become clear in this process and our children learn to accept both aspects, increasing their awareness of their responsibility for the welfare of everyone in the community (family) including themselves.

RELATIONSHIPS

As our children reach school age, their experience of community begins to change. The community itself expands beyond the family and it is our job as parents to help children become an integral part of these larger communities. We need to provide them with expectations for their behaviour, in addition to an understanding of their interdependence with those around them. The teaching of your family values (honesty, generosity, patience and compassion) can easily be overlooked amidst the day-to-day activities but this can happen at great expense. When we cultivate virtues in our children, it gives them tools to improve their relationships with themselves, the family and others at large.

Family discussions are a great way to help children recognize the importance of interdependence. The sharing of problems stemming from weaknesses can be seen as normal; even mom and dad have problems. Family members can use their strengths to offer help and support to other members. When celebrating a child's success, we can also remind the child to consider all those who contributed to that success: the coaches, the teammates, the teacher, the bus driver. In this way, we celebrate the child's accomplishments along with the child's interdependence.

RESPECT

One of the best ways that our children can learn this principle is by watching parents as they respond with respect to each other's needs and those of the family and the larger community. As individuals, we often idealize our partners and our family members, especially when we begin a new relationship. A new relationship, job, even a new car can be seen as the perfect solution to any problems we may have. Over time, the sparkling qualities of "new" fade and the everyday realities of the individual or the situation take over. We may feel disappointed that this person, job, car or even child did not live up to our initial idealized expectations.

This disappointment is often the source of difficulty in relationships. One key way to work past this is to see the person for who she really is. Rather than lashing out at the other person for our poor judgement of her, we can work at responding with respect and a commitment to the welfare of the other person regardless of the feelings of hurt, hatred or frustration. This doesn't mean that we ignore negative feelings and circumstances, but that we can practise assertiveness: asking for what we need using honesty and kindness rather than being aggressive and demanding what we need with no regard for the other person.

Ultimately, when we read through these five principles, the fifth leads back to the first; approaching each part of our life with a realistic or "real-life" perspective is vital to our own happiness and the teaching of that happiness to our children. These principles form a circle that moves both clockwise and counter clockwise in an effort to guide ourselves and our children to awareness of what is truly important and can give them the skills needed to weather the rocky road of life.

FEBRUARY

Star light, star bright, first star I see tonight…I wish I may, I wish I might, keep my child asleep all night.
Getting kids to sleep

My children seem to have endless energy and sometimes go into overdrive at the end of the day just as I'm getting tired and my patience is pretty much used up.–Angie, mother of two young children

Angie was not the first client to paint this picture for us. Many of us spend the first year of our child's life trying to figure out how to live without sleep. After one sleep-deprived year, we come to value sleeping over all else.

Parents tend to accept this sleep upheaval from our infants up to a point and then trust that it will go away. For many it does, only to rear its ugly head as our children enter the preschool years. All of a sudden, our child, who is now sleeping in a "big boy" bed, discovers that he is able to get up and come downstairs. What about our grownup time? CURSES! Foiled again!

GETTING READY FOR BED
At Parenting Power we work with families to help them create strategies that work for them. These tools are a great starting point for many of our clients dealing with bedtime struggles. We worked with Angie to set up a bedtime routine, as we encourage all families to do – the earlier in life the better. Angie began to view this routine as an enjoyable and lovable time for all.

A good starting point is "Bath, Brush, Books, Bed." Some families include prayers or gratitude time as well. A bedtime chart (words and/or pictures) works well for some children because they feel like they are more in control. Develop it with them and then let them check off what they need to do. Older children may want to continue to read for a certain amount of time after they have read with an adult.

Whatever the routine, consistency is the key. This is where, as parents, we have to be sure to allow plenty of time for cleanup and the routine itself, in order to get the children into bed at a decent hour. No child wants to be yanked away from an activity, told to hurry up and then thrown into bed and told to "go to sleep."

STAYING IN BED

Our little ones can't be blamed for wanting to see what they are missing when they are asleep, but we must begin to draw the line. We recommend adding the little things like a drink of water, a pre-bed trip to the toilet and the requisite number of teddy bears to the bedtime chart so that they cannot be used as excuses after the lights go out.

Children are smart and they may test new expectations/rules sometimes. But, it is most often a parent's inconsistency that allows a child to negotiate a new privilege every night. Sleep is vital to good health, happiness and learning. By being clear and concise about bedtime rules, including why sleep is so important, you will find that bedtime is much more enjoyable for all. Pleasant dreams...

Life isn't always fun
Teaching kids to survive the hardships of life

It seems that some kids nowadays don't wake up excited about the day — whatever the day. We even hear children whine about privileges, *Awww, do I have to go to hockey practice?* Hockey is a privilege! Some children seem to be losing the reverence for life itself.

Why? We suspect it is because they are learning that everything should be "fun" or have a reward at the end and when it doesn't, it just isn't worth considering or enjoying.

A recent TV program suggested that the best parenting decisions involve making things "fun" for children (and to buy their products, which helped add to the "fun"). One was a reward chart system for kids' chores and the second was a fancy plate that made eating "fun." Is it really necessary for parents to be making everything fun for kids in order to have them cooperate? Of course not!

Real life isn't always fun and children need to learn that they still need to make the best of it and get things done. In fact, if we spend all of our time working so hard to make every little thing fun, how will our children learn perseverance, responsibility and resilience?

Learning to handle life's hardships helps kids learn that they are able. Little lives typically bring little "hardships": cleaning up toys, going without that extra cookie. Learning to deal with these means learning that they can get through the big hardships that come along later: getting dumped, not getting picked for the team or job they wanted.

PARENTING WITH A PLAN
Having a plan will help you help your kid survive real life, which is not always fun.

Awareness
Recognize how much of your life is going into make chores "fun" or "entertaining." Come to an understanding about the real reasons the task needs to be done.

Eating doesn't need to be fun – we eat to live; if they are hungry, they'll eat.

Structure and consistency
When we know the reason for the task, we can then state the expectations and stick to them.

Chores are done to contribute to the family or the community because it is the right thing to do and it feels good to help others and be responsible.

Feelings
We can acknowledge our kids' feelings without needing to fix them. *I know you don't want to brush your teeth. You don't have to like it; it just needs to get done. If you want to cry, that's okay. Your health is your responsibility.*

Problem solving and autonomy
Involve the kids in the solution. We need to figure out a way for this homework to get done without whining. Let's work together to make a plan – I have some ideas and I'd like your ideas too.

Language of encouragement
Be careful not to get drawn into talking and reasoning about why a chore needs to happen. This is attention for misbehaviour. Plan a script and stick

to it. *I know you don't want to do this and I know you can. What's the next step to getting it done? Where would you like to start?*

The moral of this story is not that kids shouldn't have fun. It is that when we "make everything fun," they get distracted from realising the intrinsically great parts of every day and their own ability to make it through even when things aren't fun.

Patience takes practise
Responding with respect when things get crazy

It's often easier to practise patience with people we barely know: the checkout clerk, the guy at the gas station. We maintain an air of politeness and respect and wait patiently when things go wrong, *Oh, don't worry, I have time...*

Maybe we are willing to be patient because we aren't so emotionally attached to the situation. Sometimes, the patience we most wish that we had is for those closest to us. When things don't go as planned with our family, we feel disappointed in ourselves for getting it wrong and for letting down the people we love.

It is a lot easier to practise patience with our children and ourselves when we have three important things:

- Realistic expectations of the situation.

- Realization that our children's misbehaviour isn't usually about getting at us, it is usually about something going on with them.

- Respectful language that we can use to respond when things go crazy. When we have patient words, we sound patient, we act patiently and eventually, we are patient.

Realistic expectations are something we need constantly as parents. We need to know what our children can do, and accept their limitations. From there, we can develop ways of teaching them what they need to know as they are developmentally ready to learn. Patience for this is often easier when we have little children who need us to care for them and do most things for them. As our kids mature, this can become more difficult because the child looks capable or has the words to indicate ability even if the task has not been mastered. Even our teens appear capable of logic and adult reasoning. Research now tells us that, developmentally, their brains don't see logic the way an adult does until about 25 years of age. Tricky stuff!

Secondly, patience can be more easily extended when we **realise and remember that our child's misbehaviour is not about us**. Even though it seems like they are showing disrespect and whining and complaining about what we did wrong, when we really look behind the misbehaviour, it is likely about them. They may be feeling disappointed in themselves, frightened of failure, jealous of a sibling, anxious about an upcoming event. When we carry with us the fact that they are learning to deal with troubling situations, we can find patience to support them through the emotion and later to guide them in solving their own problems.

Lastly, we can carry a **few handy phrases** with us for these crazy occasions. When we don't have the answers or when we feel like screaming, we can say:

- *Thanks for your patience on this. I'm not sure how to figure it out but there must be a way. We can do it.*

- *Wow, we've got a problem. How can we get through this together?*

- *I see/hear that things are not working. Let's find a new way to work this out.*

- *Wow, I am feeling panicky here. There must be a way to get some calm…*

Patience is about being gentle with yourself and others when things aren't going as planned. Find one way to practise patience today. Your kids will see it and learn from you.

A dirty little parenting secret many of us share
Liking one kid more than another

This past week, three different parents shared a deep, dark secret with us. It took all the courage they could muster to share the same very bold secret.

Each of these parents seems kind-hearted, supportive and loving, and each of these parents told us, *Sometimes I don't like my children and I feel like it is easier to go to work than to stay home and play with them.*

When they heard that many parents feel that way from time to time and it doesn't make you a bad person, they were each so relieved. The shame of revealing this secret was almost more than each of these parents could bear. It had been a large burden, in some cases sapping energy the parent could have used in other parenting or life tasks.

There may well be many times in your life that you will love your children but you might not like them very much. If you have more than one child, sometimes you will find yourself liking one so much more than the other. This can be an awful feeling. You love them both, but one of them...well you just don't like being around him very much.

Sometimes this is an age and stage thing. As one of your children grows out of that stage, becoming likeable again, the other sibling often grows into it so you can dislike him for a while. Sometimes it may be due to a temperament that doesn't fit with your personality: often the things we like least about someone else are the very same things we can't stand in ourselves.

Perhaps you are struggling with really getting through to that child or she knows exactly the buttons to push you over the edge.

Another way that this scenario plays out is that your strengths and weaknesses don't align with those of your child. If you are a very sedentary person and your child is all about athletics, it might be really hard for you to run around and play at the park with her. What if you are a tom-boy and your daughter is a girlie-girl who only wants to play fairies and make-believe? Or what if you hate the water and your child only wants to swim and splash?

It can feel pretty disappointing when the vision you had of the parent you were going to be or the child you were going to have gets shattered like a plate glass window with a baseball. It's pretty tempting to sit in the pit of despair doing one of the following:

- Blaming yourself for not being a good enough parent

- Pushing your child to be the child you always wanted, not letting him be who he is

- Setting yourself up to fail by forcing yourself to do stuff you hate in the hope that you will learn to love it or punish yourself enough that you can stop feeling shame

So how do you pull yourself out of the pit? Spend a bit more time there to really know what you are doing there in the first place. Take a look around so that you can remember it because, hopefully, it is now time to allow yourself out!

Recognize the expectations you had set for yourself in terms of the parent you were going to be. Did you even have a clue what parenting was about when you set those expectations? Begin to create expectations that are more in line with who you are now (strengths/weaknesses; likes/dislikes).

Know who your child is right now. This doesn't mean that she will be this way forever – she might or it might be something that changes by next week. If you really don't like her very much, see if you can create a list of five things that you do like about her. If you can't do this, start to ask people around you for help because it is important to have some positive thoughts for when you have nothing good to say.

Once you can accept the child you have right now, take a look at the strategies that your child needs to learn. (Is she constantly forgetting stuff? Let's guide her to learn strategies so that she can remember.) Make a plan to teach these strategies, slowly – we need to set her up for success.

STOP punishing yourself by making yourself do the stuff you hate. If you don't like playing princess, but love to have a dance party – plan a daily dance party together and then let your daughter play princess on her own (or set the timer and only make yourself play princess for five minutes). Kids need to learn independent play.

The more we see people (and ourselves) as they (we) really are, the easier it is to have an honest relationship. It is hard work pretending to be who we aren't. It is hard to be constantly disappointed by what isn't.

What's more, who we are will be different six months from now – then we'll have to get used to that new person all over again. Get out of the pit, let yourself off the hook and have some fun...life's too short.

Oh yeah, one more thing...find a trustworthy person who loves you more than you do – when you are feeling so shameful about something that it is burning a hole in your heart, please tell that person. He or she will continue to love you and you may find out that it's a secret we all share.

MARCH

WEEK 9   **Winning and losing**
Teaching good sportsmanship

WEEK 10   **Spring Break survival**
Realistic tips for a week of family togetherness

WEEK 11   **Discipline**
Teaching responsibility

WEEK 12   **Story time for parents**
Using self-talk to change negative parenting

Winning and losing
Teaching good sportsmanship

Have you ever let your child win a game because it was just easier than letting him lose? The world loves a winner and why wouldn't we want our child to feel like a winner?

Actually, there is a reason: this is real life and our children won't always be winners; none of us are. It is important that your child learn how to win and lose with grace. Good sportsmanship applies to all aspects of life where we compete with others or measure our success by comparing ourselves with others.

When kids are sore losers, or rude winners, other children don't like playing with them. One of our parenting jobs is allowing our kids to lose and learn that they can get through it.

Annual sporting events give all of us a chance to celebrate the winners, the losers and the team players. This is the perfect time to teach your kids to win and lose gracefully.

1. **Plan the end of the game before you start playing.**
   Before you start that game of checkers, have a conversation.
   At the end of this game, someone is going to win and someone is going to lose. The last time you lost, there was lots of screaming. What will you say this time when you feel sad? What will you say if you win?

2. **Just before the end of the game, review the plan.**
   Practise what to say.
   If you win, you are going to say — Great game mom, thanks for playing!
   If you lose, you will say — I wish that I had won, thanks for the game of
   checkers. If you feel like you need to, you can do five jumping jacks to get
   your mad out.

3. **Check how important winning really is in your family.**
   Kids learn what they live. If every game is about who wins, they will
   learn how important winning is. Be aware of the messages you are
   sending. Do you tweet, post and brag about your child's wins? If all
   we talk about is their external accomplishments, then our kids think
   and live like those are all that matters.

4. **Are you the parent who explodes when the ref makes a
   wrong call?**
   If you are so wrapped up in whether your child's team wins or
   loses, maybe it is time for you to work off some steam at your own
   extra-curricular activity. Our kids' activities are about them learning
   skills, teamwork, winning and losing. Most of all, they are about
   having fun.

Spring Break survival
Realistic tips for a week of family togetherness

Some parents love Spring Break: no need to drive kids to activities, kids are home to help with the chores, and it's a great excuse to "not work" and have fun. Some parents, however, DREAD this time. It means finding time off work, having the kids bugging them all week, finding stuff for the kids to do and dealing with the complaints that they're the only kids in their classes who are not headed to Mexico or Disneyland.

What if you have decided to go on vacation with your children? We encourage you to be realistic about the experience – travelling with kids can be fun, exhausting, adventurous, hair-raising, frustrating and memorable...and that's just in the first day of the trip.

Here are some tips to help you, whether you are staying here or getting away.

- **Plan for sleep**
  When we take away sleep from kids and adults, they get cranky. This may seem obvious but it is amazing how often it surprises parents. If your kids want to stay up late (or they will because of your schedule), set expectations for naps or sleeping in. If your son rises predictably at 6:30 am no matter when he goes to sleep, be clear about what bedtime will be from the start, and STICK TO IT!

- **Plan for real life**
  If you are staying home this Spring Break, groceries, laundry, dishwashing, etc., all still need to get done. Set yourself up for success by

planning when these will happen, and letting kids know the schedule and how they are expected to help (pitching in or independent play while you take care of it).

If you are going away, real life means that part of your family will not want to go to the Museum of Ear Wax, while others will want to spend the whole day there. Perhaps you do not want to spend 24/7 at the hotel pool and would like to get out and see some sights. Talk about schedules, working together (or splitting up – one parent gets a free day while the other stays with the kids) and attitudes ahead of time (consequences included).

PLAN FOR MEALS AND BEHAVIOUR

Staying home

Will there be play dates, visits to a wave pool or the library? Discuss behaviour expectations and consequences. In addition, there is a good chance that your children cannot/will not want to spend every waking moment together. Schedule quiet times, times for independent play and teach scripts for when your kids need a break: *I need some time in my room please, I'll play with you again in 30 minutes* (vs. *I hate you, get out of my face!*).

Going away

Discuss expectations for behaviour at the restaurants, pools, hotel lobby, etc. (Don't forget consequences as well). While we are on the topic of restaurants, it is very easy, when your kids eat off children's menus, to have children eating cheese and starch at every meal: pancakes for breakfast, grilled cheese at lunch, pizza for dinner. If that works for you, great! If not, outline the expectations for the number of fruits/vegetables to be eaten each day, how many sugary treats they can have and whether dessert is a "for sure" thing at each meal. Please schedule down time for your kids. They will need it...you will need it.

Technology: Can they live without it? Can you?

Getting away from technology can be one of the hardest things to plan nowadays. "Why would I want to?" you ask. That's up to you. If your goal is to spend family time together or you want your kids to have some physical exercise so that they don't drive you batty, set limits up front. If they choose to observe the limits, they can continue to use technology; if not, they're choosing to go without for the day. Kids learn what they live so if you expect them not to text while talking to you, model that when you are talking to them.

This list could go on forever and we're happy to help you if you have any questions.

CONSEQUENCES

One last suggestion would be in the department of consequences. Consequences need to fit your child and the misbehaviour. Use language to help you find just the right consequence.

I see running and hear shrieking. Your behaviour shows me you are choosing to leave the pool for today and skip it tomorrow. You can try again the next day. I know you are capable.

When you choose to use quiet voices, walking feet and keep your hands to yourselves, you are choosing to stay at the restaurant. When you choose not to do this, you are choosing to sit with me in the car.

This is only a valid consequence if the child wants to stay in the restaurant. If your child is sick of you and is dying to be on his own, either create an opportunity for some down time for him or have him sit right beside you so you can "help" him when he does not control his hands.

You are choosing to hit your brother — this means that you are choosing to have me help you to control your hands. When you are ready to try again, let me know and I'll let go.

You are getting filled up on sweet treats, so you are choosing to skip those tomorrow and fill your body with healthy foods. When you show us you can do that, we'll go back to a treat once the healthy food has been eaten.

PRACTICAL MATTERS

Lastly, if you are travelling this holiday, be realistic and clear with your kids about airports, car trips, hotels and so on. Travelling is not always fun. Security people may not have a sense of humour. Talk about the rules; for example, what cannot be said out loud in an airport. It might be a good idea to create a "Try to use the bathroom whenever we actually find one" rule. It can also help to pack a change of clothes for every family member in re-sealable freezer bags so that when someone spills a drink, or throws up on you, you will have something to wear (and an extra change of clothes if the airlines lose your luggage). If your kids packed their own carry-on bags, please check through them for water guns or other "weaponry" that airport security will not appreciate.

Here's hoping you have a wonderful week, here or away. Be realistic and remember... if you make a mistake when your kids misbehave, you will always get another chance to do it right, possibly in the next 20 minutes.

Discipline
Teaching responsibility

The origins of the word "discipline" are from the Latin *disciplina* (teaching) and *discipulus* (pupil). While many people see discipline as having a negative connotation, at Parenting Power we believe that discipline is about teaching. We teach our children how to make good choices so that when they are on their own they will use self-discipline and learn from their mistakes. They will see themselves as people who know how to make choices and they will know that every choice they make will have consequences (positive or negative).

Many of us know people who grew up in families where the parents made all of the decisions. As children, these people were told that everything was fine and that there was nothing to be upset about even when they were upset. These kids were never allowed to make a choice in case they made the wrong one and got hurt (physically or psychologically). The parents protected their children from difficult situations and "bad" friends, choosing instead to make all the decisions for their children. This was done with the best of intentions to protect little Suzy or Johnny.

Unfortunately, this meant that Suzy and Johnny grew up to be Sue and John who didn't have a clue how to make a decision. This drove their friends crazy when it came time to choosing from a menu or deciding which movie to see. But it really hampered Sue when she married Bill. She didn't really love him, but married him because, "He seemed like a nice enough guy…my parents really liked him." Sue and Bill got divorced within two years. She had never learned how to make big decisions as a kid so this was the first time she learned the consequences of making her own decisions.

John suffered a lot when he invested in what seemed like a pretty reasonable plan to put his name on a mortgage for a guy who couldn't get his own. He was told he would get 30 per cent profit when they sold the house. The guy "Seemed like a friendly sort of guy." John was left with a house in his name that he can't really afford. The friendly guy is long gone. John never learned the bad friend lesson on his own because his parents protected him from it.

The temptation to protect our children from hurt and suffering as they head off to school is strong. As parents, safety is our number one priority. However, we need to learn to balance this with supporting our children as they learn what will happen when they make poor choices. When our kids are little, the falls are small; the costs of these lessons are quite tiny. There is a form of inflation that occurs if we wait to let our kids learn lessons. The examples above show that the cost of learning how to make a decision or choose a good friend can be excessive as our kids grow into adults and make their first mistakes with their finances, friendships and life choices.

This lesson screamed from the front pages of the newspaper this morning: hundreds of snowmobilers were caught in an avalanche, with two men being killed leaving behind children and family members who will never be the same. This loss of life is a tragedy. The telling part of this story (and perhaps this person was misquoted by the paper) is that a family member asked why someone didn't step in ahead of time and warn the snowmobilers that this was dangerous and that there could have been an avalanche.

It has been reported that there was a High Risk Avalanche Warning in effect. Hundreds of people made the decision to attend this event despite the warning. They acknowledged that there was a risk and chose the thrill of risk-taking. Each of us has the opportunity to make these choices for ourselves. What is surprising is that this family member was waiting for a "parent" to step in and make the decision for these individuals, who were parents themselves.

Some of those who made it out safely from that weekend's disaster were interviewed later and mentioned that they had learned a lesson and will pay more attention to avalanche warnings in the future. Their learning or discipline occurred at a very inflated cost.

Bottom line: There is a clear need for each of us to learn how to make good decisions as early as we can. A skinned knee or hurt feelings may seem like a huge thing at the time but when we look at the costs of not learning those young lessons, the choice is obvious. We encourage you to take a look at the lessons you are allowing your children to discover as they grow. Discipline and self-discipline are gifts we need to give our children for their own benefit and the benefit of all who love them.

Story time for parents
Using self-talk to change negative parenting

When you hear the words "story time," do they invoke feelings of warm snuggles in a cozy spot, with your family cuddled together? Maybe "story time" causes your eyes to roll toward the ceiling thinking, *NOT that book again! We have read it so many times; I could recite it upside down and backwards!*

Many of us have had both of those story time experiences.

This week, though, we're talking about a different kind of story time; one that is ongoing. Many of us tell ourselves stories all day long. We've heard these stories in our heads so often they feel like absolute truths. These stories can be about anything; whether we are smart enough, thin enough, incapable, talented and so on.

Have you ever been on the verge of trying a new sport or hobby that seems really challenging? Many stories may have run through your mind just before trying it:

- *I'm not strong enough.*

- *I'm not in good enough shape.*

- *I'm too short* (Julie hears that story in her head all the time).

- *I don't know how to do this and I'm going to look really stupid.*

Somehow, you find the courage to do the new activity and all of a sudden there are brand new stories flying through your brain:

- *I am totally doing this!*

- *This is way easier than I thought — I guess I can do it.*

- *Wow, I can't do it yet but it is really fun working on it. I'll get it soon.*

At Parenting Power one of the things that we find amazing about self-stories is the power that they can have AND the fact that, while they seem like truth, they can almost always be changed. When we change the stories we tell ourselves, we often change our entire outlook on the situation.

Let's focus on some of the parenting stories we hear from our clients regularly.

- *My little guy is doing this behaviour just to spite me.*

- *My daughter knows how much I hate it when she whines. Why doesn't she stop it? She must be out to drive me crazy!*

- *If I were a better parent, my kids wouldn't* [insert misbehaviour here].

- *When my kids get bad marks on their schoolwork, people will think they are stupid AND that I'm stupid and a bad parent. I got really good marks in school, and I'm an idiot for not helping them to do the same.*

- *My son will be pooping in his pants forever! I have got to be the only parent around that didn't toilet train him right. I'll be doing laundry like this until he leaves for university!*

- *If I don't give in right now, my child will start screaming and we will not get through the embarrassment or the frustration! This will never change.*

- *Our kids just can't sleep through the night on their own — they never have yet so there is no point in trying.*

- *Most other parents do not yell at their kids. WHAT IS WRONG WITH ME?!*

Thankfully, at Parenting Power we know that these stories are all fiction. When we work with parents, we share a new story. It may sound like:

- *That behaviour happens with a lot of children at that developmental age and stage.*

- *We hear that story all the time and we know how to help you change it.*

When parents have a new story, they have the faith to begin again and change the old habits. Just think of the power these new stories can bring to our children! We can tell them stories that begin:

- *We had a problem and now we are working together to change it.*

- *We believe you are capable of making these changes.*

Our kids tell themselves stories all the time too. Instead of arguing with them when they come out with a negative story, see if you can notice it for what it is: *Wow, that's an interesting story you are telling yourself. Do you think that another story might work there instead?*

Once we become aware of stories that are influencing us, and the lives of our family members, we have the power to see them as just that: stories that we can rewrite and use to change the future, in the next ten minutes or over a lifetime.

Here's to loving, caring story times with your kids. And within yourself.

APRIL

What is the first step?
Choosing respect in the heat of the moment

It's fine to say that every journey begins with a single step, but sometimes that first step eludes us completely. The screaming child in the grocery store, the angry sibling who just punched her brother or the selfish teen who thinks, *You just DON'T GET IT!* Any of these moments can push us instantly past logic and reason and into a place where yelling back seems like a good first step.

Even as we react with yelling, bribing or other choice behaviours, we may see ourselves and wonder — *What am I doing?* Or, in the heat of the moment, we might not have a clue, blinded by panic, frustration, shame, disappointment or anger. Perhaps it won't be until later when we realise what we have done — that we didn't respond with respect; we doled out too big a consequence — and we find ourselves in a situation where we are a bit shell-shocked by the events that transpired.

Here are some ways we can prepare for that first step so we don't end up repeating the same harmful responses to our kids' habits.

1. **See the habit for what it is.** If this misbehaviour has happened before, you may feel even more frustrated. It may feel like your child is showing disrespect by doing it again after you told her not to last time. This may add to the emotion of your response. We follow the Three Strikes You're Out rule — if you play out the same situation three times in a fairly short period, it is now officially a habit and you need a plan to change the habit. It won't change itself.

2. **Cut the excuses.** *He's tired. He's hungry.* Making excuses for our child's behaviour likely means we will let him off the hook this time. When we constantly make excuses, we continuously let him off the hook and the child learns that this behaviour is okay – or that the behaviour doesn't need to stop until mom or dad is screaming or threatening. Being tired and hungry may be the reasons for the misbehaviour – we can still respond by letting the child know that there are consequences for the behaviour.

3. **Plan your actions.** Knowing that you have a habit (and even in times when you don't) it is helpful to have a plan for your first steps when things go sideways. Choose something you know you can do. It might be to breathe in and out and count to three. It might be to use your body to get in between your child and another or to get to her level. If someone is being hurt, the first action step is to separate the fighting children. If in a public place, your first action might be to get out of the public eye (find a bathroom, changing room or even head to an empty aisle in the grocery store – your car is a great choice as well). If you are at home and no one is in danger of being hurt physically, you might choose to walk away from the situation initially rather than heading into it ready to let fly with a mouthful of disrespect.

4. **Plan your words.** There are so many options here and the key is finding the one that makes sense to you. The first step is usually a stall word that allows you to get your bearings and plan your next words. You might use a single word: *Wow... Gee... Okay... Whew...*

WHAT IS THE SECOND STEP?

Our next step is to let our kids know that this is not the time or the place to lose our cool. So our words need to reflect that. Yelling, blaming or shaming will not achieve this goal. Instead, you can describe and guide.

DESCRIBE words: *I see... It looks like... You seem... I hear...*

GUIDE words: *The next step is… Your behaviour is telling me you need my help… We've got a problem here, how can we solve this?*

Just having a few non-reactive words that you've planned to use can make a big difference in helping to keep your calm and then passing that calm to your child.

PREPARE YOUR KIDS AS WELL AS YOURSELF

When you are aware of your habits, you can plan new, more respectful habits and practise them. Creating and communicating clear expectations and consequences can help all family members to have success. Before you head into a situation in which old habits occurred, restate the new expectations/consequences.

You can even ask your child, *What behaviour do I expect to see in this situation? How are you going to help yourself to make good choices? What are the consequences for good choices? and for bad choices?* That way, you know that your child knows. Check in with yourself – do you have the words and actions ready? Will you know how to calmly assign the consequences rather than blaming and shaming?

As parents, we will never be able to predict our child's behaviour in every situation – that may be the source of much of our frustration. What we can do is predict our behaviour – make a plan for our actions and words. Our child's behaviour is not a reflection of our parenting. Our behaviour is a complete reflection of our parenting. If you don't like your first steps, plan new first steps so that you can feel confident, capable and calm.

The gift of mistakes
Learning from the times we mess up

Parenting is a job we take on for life. Most of us don't really have a clue what we are getting into when we first sign up. We are terrified, aroused, clueless or all of the above.

Once we are in, we're in. There's a saying, "You can't un-ring a bell," and it pretty much applies here. Even if we were to walk away from our off-spring and just keep walking and walking for days, we would still techni-cally remain a parent. There are no stat holidays from parenting, and we cannot get fired. Having spoken to parents who have suffered through losing a child, we know that even then, in that deepest, darkest of nights, one remains a parent.

While living with this tenacious assignment, we have the opportunity to practise parenting not just from time to time, but daily – actually, hourly and for many of us minute by minute. Yes, there are moments when the kids are at gymnastics, school, dance or hockey; perhaps an evening with the sitter or the grandparents, but basically, parenting is full on!

The bad news: There are multiple opportunities to make mistakes each and every time.

The good news: There's another opportunity to learn coming right along.

Making mistakes in parenting does not mean that we are failing as parents. Making a mistake is about taking the wrong path or making the wrong decision. Various definitions of the word mistake suggest that one might create an error or fault as a result of:

- defective judgement

- deficient knowledge

- carelessness

Well let's see… do any of these situations arise in parenting?

Defective judgement

Could this possibly arise from lack of sleep, burnout, overwork, the pressure to be the perfect parent, the need to outdo those around us and particularly our own parents, the unrealistic expectation to succeed at every turn, the shame, guilt, angst, anger, sorrow, disappointment, fear, helplessness, frustration that might be lurking in our hearts and minds as our child screams at full volume on the floor in front of us or is pounding on us with fists (biting us with new teeth), peeing on the good carpet, rolling eyes at us from across the room, slamming the door to the bedroom or arriving 30 minutes past curfew? That one is possible.

Deficient knowledge

Is there a chance we don't actually know what we are doing? Have any of us ever done this before with this child, in this century? Might we be lacking in experience to deal with this exact situation? Definitely possible.

Carelessness

This is not something to which many of us would want to admit but there are times when, with everything that is going on, we don't put our all into our parenting and mistakes happen.

And yet, making the wrong choice or taking the wrong path can end up leading to wonderful gifts:

- awareness

- seeking help

- gaining knowledge

ACCEPTING THE GIFT

When we find ourselves in the moment after a mistake – the sinking feeling in our stomachs, the throbbing headache, the disappointment, frustration – we are in a moment of awareness. WE CAN CHOOSE TO IGNORE OUR AWARENESS. Many of us do. That's okay too because it just means we'll land back in this hole again, maybe even later today. When we choose awareness, we know that our wrongly taken choice got us here along a yucky path, and we now have the opportunity to learn and figure out a new way so that we don't land here again.

What if we don't know what to do? Another gift…

We can seek help. Reaching out for help – from a spouse, a friend, a family member, Parenting Power or the community at large – is an act of connection. It reaffirms the interdependence of the world – the fact that we are all interconnected and part of numerous relationships. When we ask for help, the other person gets to support us by sharing a strength and hopefully compassion as well. This is the beauty of our human world.

Whichever path we choose, we end up gaining knowledge and having the opportunity to put it into action the next time this parenting challenge arises. What's more, we have struggled through and can now share compassion and suggestions with someone else who is enduring the same struggle because we are most definitely not alone in our mistake-making as parents or in any of our other roles along the way.

There is one more gift that comes from a mistake (taking the wrong path or making the wrong choice). We get to model to our children that everyone makes mistakes and that they are an opportunity for learning. We can admit our own mistakes and talk about what we learned. We can share compassion when they struggle and we can encourage them to learn from their mistakes instead of seeing mistakes as failure.

When we accept that we are not alone in our mistakes, and that they are actually a requirement for growth and knowledge, we are making a great parenting choice.

Cyberbullying
Facing the problem as a family

We are hearing more and more about cyberbullying. The media seems to be asking, *What can schools do about cyberbullying? What is the government doing about this situation?*

At Parenting Power we have one question: *What are you, as a parent, doing about this situation?*

Because this is the cold hard fact about our current reality: Each family needs to step up and take responsibility to stop this from happening in the future. We need to bring the responsibility back to the home and not make it the government's job or the school's job. IT IS OUR JOB.

Here's what we all need to do:

- Teach our boys and girls about the way to treat people with respect and to expect respect.

- Hold our kids accountable and responsible for their whereabouts when they are not with us. This doesn't mean that we trace their cell phone GPS. It means that we make sure that they are where they say they are. It means that rather than hoping they aren't getting into trouble, we know that they aren't. It means that they are held to consequences when they make the wrong choices.

- Stop being bystanders when stuff happens on our street or in our school playgrounds or at the mall. When we watch someone mistreating another and do nothing about it, we are essentially joining the wrong-doer. We are also teaching our kids to do the same. We all need to take responsibility for stepping in or at least getting help for the victim.

- Teach our boys and girls that rape is not an option.

- Teach our kids what to do when they receive a demeaning picture or post on their technology devices. We need them to know that, at the very least, they need to delete it. Ultimately, they should also report it. They cannot send it forward!

This education begins when our kids are little and continues as the children grow. It is intentional parenting – knowing what we want to teach and making a plan to teach it. Sometimes it will be a conscious decision (when we are teaching kids about internet safety and courtesy; or discussing expectations when they get their Smartphone).

More often, it will be when we are living our values because, make no mistake, our children are watching us – 75 per cent of what they learn comes from watching us – from our actions. Kids live what they learn and learn what they live.

If you already have older children, talk to them about rape. Talk to them about rape jokes and how they aren't funny. Teach them how to respond when their buddies demean women. Teach them how to make their own choices about their actions.

If we want to prevent this situation from reoccurring, we must take responsibility. When we do this, we model for our kids that their behaviour is their responsibility; the schools and the government are not to blame. Every action begins with a choice. We need to teach our kids how to make responsible choices and that starts with us making some of our own.

Mentoring your children
Teaching problem solving

One of the toughest things about parenting is watching our children go through hardships. We cringe through teething pain when they are babies, then come the scraped knees and feelings of being left out when "everyone got invited to the party but me." What we really want to do is to take the pain away. For a while, a parent's kiss has a magical quality, but magic doesn't last forever.

When the kiss stops working, and the Band-Aids don't carry as much allure as they once did, our next instinct is to take on our children's problems. We try to solve them by giving orders or asking a multitude of questions:

- *Don't be rude to your friends!*

- *Take that late homework to your teacher first thing in the morning and apologize for not handing it in yesterday!*

- *Why did you hit Grant? How would you feel if he had hit you?*

- *Why didn't Susan invite you to her party? Were you mean to her?*

Problem solving for our children can seem like a kind and caring way to parent but it sends a conflicting message. It may seem loving, yet the actions say, *Let me solve your problems for you because you aren't capable of solving them yourself.*

When we have infants in our home, this is reality – they need us to bathe, feed, change and care for them. But, as these infants develop into preschoolers and beyond, we have an opportunity to mentor them – to teach them how to solve their own problems. When they are young, their problems are often small ones. What better place to begin learning how to look after one's self?

A mentor can be defined as a person charged with the instruction and guidance of another. When we seek out a business mentor, we aren't looking for someone to do our work for us, we are seeking guidance with what we strive to do for ourselves. Bringing this model into the parenting situation can be helpful and rewarding.

- **Provide boundaries and then give children the freedom to act within those limits.**
  When our children make choices for themselves, they begin to see themselves as decision makers.

- **When your child asks you a question, find out his opinion before giving your answer.**
  This encourages independent thinking and lets you know more about what he was asking and where he's headed. It also implies that you are interested in his opinion and that you believe he can generate worthwhile solutions.

- **Meet your children where they are.**
  Acknowledge that new tasks can be difficult and encourage their effort with small steps: *Wow, pouring your own milk from that big jug can be hard on the arms. Why don't I put that into a smaller pitcher and then you can give it another try?*

- **Create opportunities for self-discovery.**
  When starting a new craft project or heading out on a neighbourhood walk, invite your child to explore the materials or choose the path.

- **When your child asks a question that you aren't sure how to
  answer, help her find an expert to answer the question.**
  Growing children ask interesting, deep questions that can have
  far-reaching implications. Teaching them to seek out answers from
  qualified experts can have many positive results. It teaches them that
  not knowing all of the answers is acceptable in your family (no one
  needs to be perfect, mistakes are okay).

There are many resources to help us find an answer to our questions. As a
parent, you support your child in finding answers to questions that she may
not feel comfortable asking you.

When the life-impacting questions come around a little later on and your
child is embarrassed to ask you, she will be thankful to have learned how
and where to find truthful answers to these questions and will have the
confidence to do so. As a parent, you may never know that she sought help,
but you will know that she is capable.

Being a mentor–parent means taking the time to teach your children and
asking questions that will help them to find answers to their own problems.

Lost for words: How to stay afloat when the ground turns to quicksand
Answering your child's tricky questions

Somehow we manage to get used to the change of having our children in preschool and find ourselves actually enjoying it. Then one day, our purest-of-thought-little-angel comes home and utters a bad word, a bad thought or (and here comes the quicksand) a question like, *Dad, Suzy told me that I came from mommy's tummy? How did I get there?*

Suddenly, the world starts spinning and it is hard to stay standing. You imagine yourself saying, *Actually precious, the stork brought you,* or *Well, it was a cold November morning when we found you under the cabbage leaves.* You always thought of yourself as an honest parent who wanted to educate your child in the facts of life in a matter-of-fact way. But now…where do you start?!

STALLING TECHNIQUES 101
One of the easiest ways to regain your footing and your ability to speak is by using a stalling technique. These come in handy when dealing with all sorts of parenting questions from preschool to university. They give some time to gather your wits, seek out information and teach your child that even adults don't know everything but are happy to do some research.

1. **Begin your stall with an encouragement for asking a good question:**

- *That's a great question.*

- *I'm really glad that you asked that.*

2. **Follow that with a clarification:**

- *So you're asking me…*

- *Where did you hear that?*

- *What else did Suzy say?*

- *So what do you think?*

3. **Finally, buy yourself some time:**

- *Okay, let me see, where should I begin?*

- *Hmm, now what is the best way for me to explain that?*

- *I don't know – I can check into it for you though.*

- *Sounds important – why don't I check with mom/dad and see when we can talk about this as a family.*

Having caught your breath and landed yourself an opportunity to discuss these questions with your co-parent (or anyone else for that matter), you can develop a plan for how to answer these questions honestly and with information relevant to your child's level of development.

Discussing these and other issues with honesty and some sense of comfort during the preschool years can set a wonderful model for honest communication in the future when we will really need it. If you are looking for answers, there are great books to read and we offer courses on this very topic as well. Preparing yourself to answer these kinds of questions can get you and your child out of quicksand, now and in the future.

MAY

A calm spring
Creating a pace of life that fits your family

As the days grow longer and the earth reawakens, there seems to be a quickening of step. Warmer weather means fewer layers and it is much easier to get outside and enjoy the freedom afforded with the coming of spring. The birds are everywhere, the blossoms and leaves are emerging and we are carried away with all that surrounds us. It's almost like a Disney movie, in which the princess sings out the windows to the animals and everyone pitches in to start working and clearing out the old of winter, making room to welcome in the new.

There are, however, other perspectives of spring that may also enter the picture: spring hockey, spring cleaning, gardening, soccer, baseball, tennis, basketball, dance exams, piano exams, provincial achievement tests, final exams, family barbeques, camping, get-aways, graduations, end of year banquets, swimathons, skipathons, marathons, triathlons. STOP!!! Spring can be an incredibly busy time of year and it is easy to get swept along in the path of all of these events without even realizing it.

If you are busy and your kids are busy, there is a good chance that the ideas of calm and spring cannot even be mentioned in the same breath. It is easy to get caught up in all of the things surrounding us as a family. It happens at various times throughout the year and it can seem almost as if it is out of our control.

- *It's not our fault – these things all just happen at the same time.*

- *Mike loves to play hockey and soccer but choir isn't over yet so we just have to dig in and get it all done.*

When something goes wrong at home, it is not uncommon to hear children answer with *It's not my fault…* At Parenting Power we respond to this statement with *It's not about blame. How can we take responsibility to make sure it doesn't happen again?*

This is a great time to take responsibility to make sure that what is happening in our lives is the way we want it to be. If not, we always have an opportunity (and some would say an obligation) to change it.

The first step to change is awareness – an awareness of what is happening right now and what parts of it don't fit with the values and needs of your family and its members. Some suggestions for awareness are:

1. **Build a list of "calm" activities that you have pictured for your family during the spring and summer.**
   This may include things like longer walks through parks or your neighbourhood, visiting with other families, gardening, doing crafts and spending time together.

2. **Determine how realistic this dream list is.**
   If you have always dreamed of cycling to a remote area with the family, is that realistic when your youngest is still on training wheels? Dream lists are great but let's stick with calming activities your family can actually accomplish without the need for swimming lessons or teaching someone how to roller blade.

3. **Build a list of all of the activities that are currently taking your time and stopping you from the activities in point 1.**
   One of the greatest time-thieves of our generation is technology. Keep a family log for one week of how much "free time" is spent with technology. Have each family member track technology time

per day. This may give you a great place to cut back and build in some of the activities from your first list.

When we take responsibility for our own sense of calm and happiness, we model this for our children. We show them that rather than being carried along with the big group, we can stop, assess the situation and make changes that work for our family. This is exactly what we want our kids to do when things aren't going well on the playground, at school and everywhere along the way in their lives.

Awareness also helps us to see where our expectations are way out of touch with reality. Whenever this happens, guilt begins to grow and that can really get in the way of our parenting. Creating realistic expectations is a great way to decrease the guilt and feel better about what you are doing in life.

Bottom line: It is great to have dreams for our family and our lives together. Sometimes, those dreams are beyond our reach. The only way to get even close to them is to be aware of the current situation and to begin to move the reality somewhat closer to those dreams one step at a time.

We wish you some calm this spring to envision what the baby steps might be, even if they don't get here until summer.

Is life really like that?
Every family struggles. There are no perfect parents.

How do we know that something is real? Most of us trust the adage "seeing is believing." Of course, we know that with the ability to alter images nowadays, a picture might not be completely accurate; almost everyone knows that the images we see on magazine covers have been touched up, slimmed down or enhanced in some way.

When we really stop to think about it, and engage a purely logical mind, we know that many images presented to us via the media are not real. In fact, the happy families we see in magazines are rarely related. They may just be four models who were paid, posed and asked to look really "happy" for the picture. We see one picture out of many shots taken – the one picture in which everyone was looking at the photographer and smiling just so.

Photographs in magazines and ads are used to evoke feelings and save writers a thousand words. So, even though you might be aware that it is not real, your eyes see the picture and it generates a feeling, maybe even a few beliefs about future possibilities.

Let's take it a step further. A large proportion of North American parents today grew up watching TV. Depending on your age, you might have watched Gilligan's Island, Happy Days, Love Boat, The Cosby Show, All My Children or any number of other programs. These shows had characters that were somewhat like us – we could relate to them in some way. They were living-imaginary-friends. In most shows, things were pretty nice

– rooms were well decorated, moms and dads got along, even if there were problems, they were usually resolved in 30 minutes (actually 22 minutes if you don't count the commercials). Once resolved, the problems never came back because the following episode was about a new problem.

We may not have known it then as kids, but we certainly know now – television isn't real. But when we were formulating our plans for the kinds of parents we would be or the kinds of families we would have, there is a good chance that this un-real way of life worked its way into our dreams just like the altered images of cover models still make us want to look that good in a swim suit or make us want to drive that amazing sports car because that will make our lives so much better.

This is where we ask that question again – how do we know that something is real? Our bodies/minds start to believe what we see on a regular basis. We may begin to think that somewhere, there are families that have it all together like they did on TV. We suppose that there are kids who don't ever misbehave and who always eat what is put in front of them.

We may even wonder:

- *Am I the only parent I know who loses it and yells at my kids?*

- *Are my kids the only ones who don't go to bed and stay there?*

- *How did we turn into one of those families when everyone else seems to be making it work?*

When our realities don't match the dreams we had, we can feel a number of emotions – anywhere from frustration and disappointment to shame and guilt. Often, the next step is to want to keep these feelings a secret from our friends – if they really knew how we were feeling, they wouldn't want us around them anymore.

If we found the courage to share some of these feelings with a truly close friend, one who wouldn't judge and would support us, we might find out that the one friend gets it because that friend is living a pretty similar life to our own. Perhaps her kids do eat their veggies but she and her spouse cannot figure out how to get their daughter to sit quietly in class and their 12-year-old son to stop back-talking his dad.

We might find out that life is not really the way it was on TV. That it is grittier and more complex. That it takes more than 22 minutes to create a problem, laugh about it, find the perfect solution, put it into practice and head out for ice cream with the perfect joke being shared around the table, the Fonz saying "aaaeeeyyy" and a laugh track bubbling up just as the final theme song plays on the juke box.

We might find out that there are some amazing events right here in real life – really interesting arguments/discussions that take place around the dinner table or success as our kids persevere and ride the two-wheeler. What about that knowing look between spouses when our child does something incredibly cute or incredibly frustrating? That is real life too.

TOOLS FOR REAL-LIFE PARENTING
1. Recognize the feelings that arise when our expectations are out of whack with reality and the actions that accompany them:

   - Getting really quiet and feeling like you are the only one

   - Judging/blaming those around you when they don't live up to the expectations

2. Share your feelings with a close friend or your partner. Find out whether your expectations are realistic; are you the only one?

3. Develop more realistic expectations for yourself, your child or your family around that situation.

4. Create some language to support you as you move through this process:

- *This is real life – I can handle this feeling.*

- *I know how I will respectfully respond to this misbehaviour.*

Living in the real world is a lot easier when we are living with real-life expectations for ourselves. Once we begin to accept our own strengths and weaknesses, it is much easier to model that for our kids and to develop realistic expectations for them as well. Realistic expectations, that are age-appropriate and that allow struggle and challenge, frustration and disappointment help us to create an environment in which our kids can learn. That is real life.

Success
What does it look like for you?

At Parenting Power we help parents to create success at home. We know that our children learn from watching us and our actions. One of the best ways to further a feeling of success and esteem is to set ourselves up for success.

Some of our greatest parenting frustrations arise from having unrealistic expectations of our children. We need to see our children for who they really are, not who they were six months ago or where they may be six months from now. When we see them in the here and now, our expectations will meet their cognitive, social, emotional and physical development. When they are capable of meeting these expectations, our children feel confident and have the courage to try even harder.

This same growth occurs when we allow them to do that which they are capable of doing. If they were struggling with a zipper two months ago, they may have aced it by now. But if we continue to zip up their coat, we are demeaning them – yes, literally de-meaning them (taking away their sense of meaning or self) and not allowing them to feel their own small successes.

Success is a process, a collection of small steps along the way. This is especially true with parenting. Our society is so focused on instant gratification and yet parenting doesn't always give us that immediate positive feedback. We will all have our stumbles, perhaps several each day. If we stop and judge ourselves each time we falter, we might never feel confidence.

Many parents spend hours of their lives reminding themselves, in fact berating themselves for what they didn't do — what wasn't checked off the list (mental or paper). Taking a moment each day to remind ourselves of what we did accomplish — feeding our kids, keeping them safe and clean, driving them where they needed to be, supporting our family members, meeting our own needs, laughing together and loving those around us — brings a daily reminder of success and an opportunity to model this process to our children.

This is not to say that we shouldn't be aware of our challenges. Learning from our mistakes benefits us all. This awareness enables us to see where we can go. With that vision, we can create a way of getting there — of teaching ourselves and our children what we want to see and how to get it. When we give clear instructions outlining what we expect, we set our children up for success and in return reap the rewards ourselves.

For example, telling our children to clean their rooms may be the first step in a huge argument when their version of clean and ours do not align. When we clearly explain that books need to be on the shelf, toys go in the basket, pens and paper in the desk and clothes in drawers or hampers, we are creating clear expectations. A checklist or a series of photos of the clean room can help our children even more by teaching them the process of achieving what we expect. In addition, hooks that they can reach themselves, pictures and words on toy boxes and clothing drawers can help them to feel even more independent and successful.

With confidence comes the courage to try. When we recognize our children's capabilities, and encourage them, our children gain courage to grow. They know that when they stumble, they can pick themselves up and try again. They also learn that from watching us when we stumble. If we allow ourselves to make mistakes and to learn from them, our children learn that they can do that too.

In closing, we recently asked a number of parents when they feel most successful. The responses were as varied as the people we asked, but each brought a smile to our faces. Here are some of them. We encourage you to think about when you feel most successful as a parent.

What makes you feel successful as a parent?

- *Time — when I stop looking at my emails, and I am conscious. I am very aware of the time that I spend with them every single day.*

- *When I tap into calling them to a value. This keeps me calm; it reminds me what I want from them and what I don't want from them.*

- *When I can model that I am sharing my skills with people who need my help through community work.*

- *When my kids tell me, "I love you Mommy."*

- *When I watch my children parent their children successfully.*

- *When my 15-year-old daughter was able to pay for a trip to England for herself through hard work, while maintaining good grades.*

- *When I see how happy my children are as adults and when I watch them successfully deal with the times that they aren't happy.*

Success is different for every one of us. Take a moment to consider your expectations for success and enjoy the process of getting there.

Mother's Day resolution – Don't be too nice.
Teaching independence

Mother's Day brings with it thoughts of flowers and brunch, cards and artwork; wonderful ways to recognize moms and thank them for their efforts year-round. As mothers, we may feel elated at the treatment or wonder just how much will be left for us to clean up once it is done.

Parenting Power's gift to moms the world over is a suggestion for moms: **Don't be too nice.**

Yes, that's right – Stop being too nice to your kids. It isn't helping them.

What are we talking about?!

Well, let's start with your toddler, the one who tantrums whenever he doesn't get that treat at the grocery store. When you are a "Nice Mom" and give him the treat because, after all, it's not his fault he gets dragged out for groceries each week, you are really teaching him to tantrum to get what he wants.

What about your preschooler who won't eat her dinner unless there is a sugary treat for dessert? "Nice Moms" give their kids sugar every day because it makes them happy, right? WRONG! It increases the amount of unhealthy sugar in her diet (which is not helping her) and it teaches her that she can negotiate for the right bribe because you are worried that she won't eat her dinner and will be hungry.

Next it is the school-age child who gets another electronic device because it will make him happy. All of his friends have them so really it's the nice thing to do. How is all of this stuff helping him to become a kind, caring, active, generous, independent human being? How is the daily argument to turn off the device/computer/TV helping your relationship? It isn't.

What about the teen who is struggling with her homework? You nicely help her with her project and email the teacher to ask for an extension just to help her out. You do her chores for her because she has a big test coming up and needs the time to study. NO – when you nicely put yourself between your teen and her problems, you become the problem. She needs to learn how to ask the teacher for help. She needs a chance to schedule her life with time to get chores and studying done. You already passed high school – now it is her turn.

Go ahead; be nice to your kids this Mother's Day and every day. Just don't be too nice – you will kill them with kindness.

Surviving parenting storms
Managing misbehaviour

You might not be old enough to remember a sitcom of our childhood – The Facts of Life. If you do remember it, the theme song has probably already begun playing in the back of your mind as you continue to read this article. Why does it matter? This past weekend and, in fact, this past while, the antics of our children have left us fuming – as every parent does from time to time.

As you may remember, the theme song begins: "You take the good, you take the bad, you take them both and there you have – The Facts of Life…"

Thankfully, as parents, we get the good and the bad. Otherwise, it couldn't be done.

Opposites are useful – very useful. Looking for the calm gets us through the storm, and sometimes the storm helps us to appreciate relative calm. If we spend our days, our weeks, our years wishing away the storms whenever they happen, then we will have wasted days, weeks and years of our lives.

Storms happen. Children will misbehave – it's what they do; how they learn what they need to learn. Some of our greatest learning moments have come from our biggest falls – giant, whopping mess-ups. Yes, our parents did warn us ahead of time, but sometimes the real message only cracks through the skull when a little embarrassment or real-life consequences help it through.

Knowing that our children are normal – that these misbehaviours and mistakes are supposed to happen – can make it just a little easier to take. Knowing that parents and kids have the opportunity to learn from mistakes is even better.

So the next time you have to take the bad along with the good, here are a few things to keep in mind:

- *Just because my child is acting like a goof doesn't mean I'm a bad parent. My child is an individual living his own life, making his own choices and learning from his mistakes if I allow him to learn.*

- *I can allow my child to make mistakes so that he can learn.*

- *I can support my child when things go wrong – I can get her through the emotional turmoil and once things have calmed down I can allow the real consequences to occur and then ask her what she would do differently next time. If she doesn't know, we can work it out together.*

- *One part of learning from mistakes is figuring out how to make amends.*

- *My child is not doing this stuff just to get at me – most of the time he isn't even thinking about me, he's doing his own thing.*

- *How I respond to my child's mistakes says a lot about my parenting.*

- *If, as a family, we keep replaying the same mistakes, we need a new plan. We can work out a new plan or we can get some help.*

Who knew a theme song could be so inspiring? Spring is in the air – kids have got spring fever. Start making a plan to handle things that come along so that you can stay confident, capable and calm.

JUNE

Normal
Accepting our faults

A mom leaned in to one of us this morning and told one of her most deeply guarded secrets. It took 25 minutes of conversation, and a revelation of something somewhat personal on our end, before this sacred item could be uncovered. The only way we can possibly feel okay about retelling this secret to you is to make it anonymous. You must never know the true identity of this woman.

Here is the secret that she shared in carefully measured increments to be sure that she would not be judged any more than necessary: she yells at her kids.

That's right! She is a mom of two kids under five years of age and she yells at them. This is something she had a hard time saying aloud. The best part: She was very relieved to know that a) we could help her come up with some new strategies and b) SHE IS NORMAL!

One January, a group of preschool parents got together for a parenting workshop. These ladies, all strangers, had only their preschool in common. When we asked them to share their current challenges, one mom alone was brave enough to raise her hand. She quietly told us that although her daughter was in preschool and was supposed to be toilet-trained, her daughter wasn't quite trained – she wore pull-ups to school. This mom felt awful that her child was the only one. One by one, the moms in the circle told how their child was also not toilet-trained and they thought that they were the only one. Suddenly, the grey clouds lifted and the realization that there were others sharing similar experiences brought everyone together.

We talk to countless parents each week. While each family is unique and every human has their own enigmatic qualities, almost every family we talk to tells us exactly the same thing and says it under the veil of shame and the promise of silence. They yell at their kids, their kids don't listen, their children fight with each other or the neighbours' kids. They don't know what to do because their child is not going to turn out right.

We're glad that parents turn to us and we are passionate about being able to help. We have dedicated the last thirteen years of our lives to doing exactly that.

The one truth that becomes ever clearer is that while each of us might be hiding some dark secret in the shadows of our being about our ability as a parent (or the lack thereof), we all have these secrets. WE ARE NORMAL. It is normal not to know the answers to every question we face. It is normal to mess some things up on a regular basis. It is normal to want to be better.

And – the only way to learn from these weaknesses is to accept that they are there and to see them in the light of day. When we look at weaknesses, it brings an awareness that they exist, that we are still okay – and gives us a starting point for change.

When we, as parents, wish to encourage self-esteem in our children, we do this through responsibility, honesty and encouraging our children to be aware of their strengths and weaknesses. Once they know that it is normal to have both sides within each of us, they can get used to good/ bad, strength/weakness, light and shadow.

As with almost everything else we teach, we need to model self-acceptance in our own lives. This means getting more comfortable with our own strengths and weaknesses. It means saying the "less than golden" stuff out loud and finding out that we are pretty normal.

There is no question that each of us carries many burdens. We live busy lives, care for aging parents or struggle at the loss of them, face the challenges of supporting our families, making the right decisions, staying healthy, exercising, eating right. These are the challenges of many of us in North America. They differ from the challenges of adults in other countries around the world. We feel gratitude and sorrow, disappointment and joy — we are normal; and normal is pretty great!

When patience isn't working
Dealing with disrespect

The way some parents practise patience doesn't seem to be working: *I wish I could be more patient. After I've asked something four times, I find myself yelling. I try to be patient but after 15 minutes of my child annoyingly thumping my back, I just lose it!*

We've heard it time and time again: Patience is a virtue. In the examples above, and many others, patience does not seem very virtuous.

When our children misbehave and we sit "patiently" by without comment, we are condoning these behaviours. Our kids will continue to misbehave to see just how long it will take before the explosion occurs.

When we repeatedly give our kids instructions (*come for dinner, set the table, pick up your coat…*) without requiring them to act, we are teaching our kids to ignore us. If they don't do it the first time (and if we don't expect them to do it the first time), then they likely won't do it until we explode. If we aren't the exploding type, then the kids will likely just wait for us to set the table or hang up the coat for them.

When we ignore a child hitting us, we are telling the child it is okay in our family to hit people.

In these situations, we are teaching our kids things that are not helping us and are not helping them either. Kids need to know that when we ask something, we expect it to be done the first time. They also need to learn how to keep their hands to themselves and to let their anger out in a way that keeps family members (and other living things) safe.

PRACTISING THE VIRTUE OF PATIENT PARENTING

When our kids misbehave, we can use self-control by not yelling or exploding. We can respond right away, clearly stating what we don't like and how it can be different.

We can be tolerant of the fact that kids will misbehave. We can make a plan to teach our kids to do things in a way that is better for the family.

We can persevere with our parenting plan, remaining consistent no matter how many times our child tests us with the misbehaviour.

We can commit to taking the time to teach our children how to behave respectfully. When we keep the vision of a responsible, capable, independent adult in our hearts and minds, we have the strength (and patience) to deal with the misbehaviours that are happening each day.

Let's rethink what day-to-day patience looks like. Here's how it could work.

Asking repeatedly

We can commit to teaching our children that we mean what we say. When we ask our kids to do something, we need to ask once and expect it to happen. Here's how to make this work. Just think **AID**: Attention, Instruction, Direction.

Attention – Go to the child and get the child's attention before asking.

Instruction – Give the instruction when standing beside the child, *I need you to set the table. Can you do it now or do you need a minute to finish what you are doing here? I can give you that minute.*

Direction – Direct the child to complete the task. If the TV remains on or the project doesn't get finished, do this for the child and then take them to the table to get it set.

If you are not in a position to follow through on the first asking, wait until you are done what you are doing and then ask for the first (and only) time. Children will learn to listen the first time and it will become a new habit.

Child hitting parent repeatedly

We need an understanding of what we will tolerate in our family around hitting/safety. Once we know the rules, we can clearly state them to our child. We need to be clear on the rule and the consequence. It could be, *When you choose to hit, you are choosing to have me control your hands. When you have control, you can try again. We can also find something safe to hit.*

The child needs to know this in advance – ideally as part of a plan (with strategies) for how to better release anger that you can work together to create.

In the heat of the moment, this becomes the way to practise patience. We hold the child's hands (or body) until he has control of them again. We may need to persevere through a tantrum, some "I HATE YOU!" moments and whatever else, in order for our child to learn that we love him and that we are taking the time to teach him the way to treat others in the family.

Patience doesn't mean accepting disrespect. When we accept disrespect, we teach our kids that it is okay to disrespect people in our family. That is not okay.

Patience works when we consistently **take time to** respectfully **teach** our kids how to show respect for all members of our family and community.

Here's to it!

Ditch that summer itch!
Facing one parenting challenge at a time

With the advent of summer, our days seem longer as the "busy" nature of our lives relents. The slower pace sheds light on issues we previously ignored. For many families the "Big ITCH" is the reminder that our kids really aren't being very nice to each other. For others, it might be that we are losing our temper more frequently, or that the chores aren't being done by the kids and we are saving them yet again.

When light gets this bright, it might be easier to just throw on some shades. Alternatively, we can take advantage of the slower pace and the bright light, take off the blinders and really look at what is going on in our own family and take steps to DITCH THE ITCH!

Is our family where we want it to be? Are our wants realistic?

What is your family's biggest itch? Now is a great time to ditch that itch; make a plan and set up some great habits while there is time and clarity to face it. It might sound daunting but you know that everyone will feel better when it is done (kind of like cleaning off the patio furniture).

Come on, let's get started. We'll even hold your hand.

1. **What is the current script that is playing out in this situation?** If it is happening regularly, there is a script... if you can't figure it out, your kids know it for sure.

2. **What do you want the situation to look like?** Until you know what you really want from the situation, there is no way you can get there. Brainstorm some possible ideas and pick the one that fits your family right now...not two years from now when your kids are older and better behaved. NOW.

3. **What limits need to be in place for that to happen?** Is it about tone of voice, clothes being in the laundry hamper, or milk cartons being flattened before they make it into the recycling container? Be clear so that your kids can understand you.

4. **What are the consequences of observing those limits AND of not observing them?** We can help you with these if you are struggling. This is not about how much pain you can inflict on your child if he or she makes the wrong choice. That's called punishment. This means...what are natural, logical outcomes of the choice they made.

   When you choose to take responsibility for your dishes – scrape them and load them into the dishwasher – you can head outside for bike riding. When you choose not to take responsibility for them, you will be here while others are bike riding...your choice.

Involving kids in steps 2 to 4 is a great idea. Just be sure that you know your bottom line first so that their ideas don't trump where you really wanted to go with this.

Shine a little summer light on your life and see what blooms.

Summer boredom and sibling rivalry
Simplifying summer routines

Summer brings a change of pace. Evenings stretch later and mornings aren't so harried. Casual calm can evolve into casual chaos! Togetherness 24/7 can be quite taxing. Emotions get out of hand and sibling rivalry skyrockets. Expecting our children to play together all the time is unrealistic, especially if they are out of practice. We feel like yelling, "CAN'T YOU TWO JUST GET ALONG?!" Well, maybe they can't.

PLANNING SUMMER ROUTINES
After ten months of life being scheduled to the minute, a lack of schedule can be really tough on children. But it also provides a great teaching opportunity for us as parents. Knowing that too much togetherness will result in disaster, we can talk with our children ahead of time about the need for each of them (and us) to spend time on our own during the day in addition to playing together. Some parents like to set this out at the beginning of the day: *We can all be together until lunch time, but after lunch, I have to do laundry and the two of you must spend some alone time until 2 o'clock. Then, let's grab the bikes and head to the pool.*

Other parents leave things more to chance, recommending alone time once behaviour goes downhill. Whatever the style, the following tips can help us set our children up for success so that they feel capable.

1. Before summer starts, set expectations around screen time, chores, responsibilities, family holidays, exercise, diet, bedtimes, curfews, etc. This is based on what matters in your family not on what happens down the street.

2. Before things go bad, explain that it's normal for them to not want to play together all of the time. Teach them to recognize and say, *I need some time to myself.*

3. Build a list of things that each child can do alone – post it in a handy location. Get supplies down from high shelves so that they don't need to bother you for them during this time.

4. Children get summers off, but whether we work from home or work in the home, our tasks continue. Communicating our needs to our children up front sets clear limits on our time. If everyone is going for groceries on Thursday mornings, build it into the schedule so that there are no surprises and fewer arguments. A posted calendar enables everyone to see what the week holds – adventures and duties alike.

LEARNING FROM BOREDOM

While keeping track of events on a calendar can be helpful, it doesn't mean that every moment of each day needs to be planned. In our society, many children are used to being entertained throughout the day. Parents often believe that they must fix boredom. In reality, our children may need help to become involved in things but they don't require constant entertainment.

Allow your children to be bored this summer; it is an opportunity for them to turn inward and away from social peers and pressure. Allowing them "nothing" time might just permit them to learn who they are, what they are actually, truly interested in, that they like spending time with themselves, that they are capable of figuring out something to do, how much time is in a day and how we choose to use it.

Boredom offers another opportunity for teaching.

For our children

Before they get bored, create a What Can I Do List. Make a list of books to read, games to play, craft projects to create, stories to write, pictures to be drawn, puzzles or word problems to solve, friends with whom to play (phone numbers too). These can take place in a tent in the backyard or in a fort in the family room.

If they aren't in the habit of independent play, start them out for a small stretch of time and then work their way up.

For ourselves

Plan a respectful response to the dreaded, *I'm BORED!* [Whining back, *If you're bored with all of these toys around, I'm going to start throwing them away!* doesn't really help.]

- *You may continue to be bored or you can find something to do from your list. I have faith that you will make the right decision for you.*

- *Perhaps your body and mind need some quiet time – why don't you check your list.*

Often I'm bored means *I need to be with you.* Acknowledge feelings and teach them to ask for some time with you instead of whining about being bored.

Lastly, when our children are home all day, we cannot totally disengage. If we tell our kids *You've got me for an hour before I have to make lunch,* then we need to provide undivided attention. Phones, computers, devices need to wait. We would expect the same of them. Multi-tasking our attention creates misbehaviour that demands our attention. Set your family up for success and enjoy the summer.

JULY

Travelling with your kids
Creating a family vacation that works

Whether across the province or the country, in a car, boat or plane, travel with children can be an "adventure" before you even leave your driveway. In our experience with our own families and the thousands we have coached, the most important thing to bring along on any trip is realistic expectations for your kids and for yourself. Once those are under control, the rest of the trip will fall into place.

Why are expectations so important? Unless you're unique, the perfect family vacation in which everyone spends all the time together and everyone gets along isn't going to happen. Realistic expectations help us to set all family members up for success both in the planning stages and in the day-to-day realities of your trip. Knowing what your kids can and will do and knowing how you will respond can be helpful when things are going as planned and absolutely essential when the trip falls off the rails. Here is a checklist of things to take into account when planning your trip and when you are on your way.

Know what your kids can handle
Do your kids love to walk and sightsee or are they more interested in the hotel pool and the closest playground? How do they do with sleeping in a new environment? Are they keen to try new foods or do they only eat what they know?

Better to plan for these things in advance rather than letting them attack when you finally arrive at your destination. If your kids love the hotel pool but you want them to see the sights, plan to divide up your time – go see the sights in the morning and then hit the pool after lunch. Bring along familiar items to help your kids get to sleep in the new bed and account for time changes as well. Pack healthy foods that you know your kids will eat or pick them up at a local grocery store. Waiting for restaurant reservations when your kids are starving can be a recipe for disaster.

Involve your kids in planning your trip

- If your kids are preschool age or younger, show them pictures of the hotel and some of the main attractions you will see.

- If your kids are school age, get them involved in researching the area or ask them what they want to do.

- Teens who are reluctant to join the family trip may feel better if they have an opportunity to plan a portion of the experience: several mornings or an event. This gives the teen some power in the situation.

Plan how you will solve disagreements that happen on the trip BEFORE you leave. Will you flip a coin? Will you act as a family, taking turns and staying involved in all activities?

Keep your own excitement level realistic as well. We want our kids to look forward to the trip but if we keep building it up to be an amazing event, the actual trip may leave everyone feeling a bit disappointed. While you are on the trip, be aware of power struggles that arise when one family member wants to do one activity and the others don't. This is a perfect opportunity to involve your kids in the problem-solving process. *Okay, we've got a problem here. I want to go to the Science Museum and you guys want to go shopping. How can we solve this together?* Maybe two groups head in two directions for the morning and meet back at the pool after 2 o'clock.

Assign realistic responsibilities based on your kids' experience and abilities

- If they are new to packing a suitcase, involve them in making the list of things to take and be sure to check after the case is packed.

- Involve them in the choice of items to take in the carry-on BUT please check it before you leave the house. It is not fun when airport security finds a toy gun in your child's bag!

- If your kids are old enough, get them their own pack to carry water, sunscreen and a book. Remember – if they can't do it, you know who will be juggling three backpacks on your walk.

How much together time can your family really handle?

- If your kids don't get along very well, create opportunities for them to do things separately on holiday.

- If you are staying with relatives on your trip, plan to be out of the house at least once every day to give everyone some down time.

- Plan in some time for one parent to be with the kids and the other to go off and explore, read a book or shop.

How are you going to respond with respect when things don't go according to plan?

- Plan to keep some tricks in your back pocket so that your behaviour doesn't add to the chaos.

- If you are in public, get you and your misbehaving child to a private place (bathroom, change room, behind the building) where you won't feel that other adults are judging you.

- If it is parent versus child, turn it into parent and child versus the situation.

- Express your feelings calmly: *I am feeling frustrated… I am disappointed with how this is going… I know we can make this work…*

- Don't fight emotion with logic. If any family members are emotional (scared, excited, mad, disappointed) use empathy to get through the emotion and get everyone to a place where they can calm down (perhaps in separate rooms). Once things are calm, then work on solving the problem.

It is no big surprise that little things blow up into big things on vacation. Sleep is often compromised, junk food and excitement are often present in higher doses than before and everyone is in cramped quarters. Knowing what you will say without blaming and shaming your kids will keep you feeling capable about how to handle bumps in the road when they occur.

Quick tips that our clients have used again and again

- For car travel, print maps so that your kids can follow along and actually tell you the answer to *Are we there yet?*

- Cookie sheets generally fit across a lap and car seat as a desk. They work with magnetic letters and the edges of the cookie sheet can stop pencils and crayons from rolling off.

- Bring snacks whether travelling by car or plane. Those unexpected delays tend to happen around mealtimes and having something with you will save you the hassle of "low blood-sugar" moments for parents and kids. Carry wipes or a wet cloth in a sealed bag for clean ups.

- Carry an extra change of clothes for everyone in re-sealable bags. If there is a spill or someone gets sick, the clean clothes are ready and the mess gets sealed in the bag.

- Whether travelling by car or plane, take advantage of every opportunity for movement. Help your kids to get the wiggles out. Play a game of follow the leader in the airport or play tag or hacky sack in a field at the side of the road. Everyone will benefit from the movement and fresh air.

- Explain to children ahead of time that whenever there is an opportunity for a bathroom break, everyone will need to try.

Keep those expectations realistic and enjoy your trip!

Learning the lessons of life
Dealing with grandparents

In a perfect world, our children's grandparents would be in good health and subscribe to the exact same parenting style we have chosen. They would be there at the drop of a hat to look after our kids and, of course, Grandma would carry caramels (or mints) in her purse. Grandpa would have the patience to sit with the little ones and tell wonderful stories of "the old days" and the kids would be over the moon at the opportunity to sit and listen.

For some families, a version of this perfect scenario exists. Many grand-parents do make the time to care for their grandchildren on a regular basis or whenever they can. In fact, many grandparents wish that they could see their grandkids more than they do. Family vacations or once-a-week mealtimes are about getting in touch with the skipped generation.

There are so many benefits to a successful "grand" relationship. The children get a chance to learn about how things used to be when the problems close at hand were war, hunger, rationing and just getting by instead of not getting into the camp we wanted, or going without the latest technology.

Often life with the grandparents moves at a slightly slower pace and there isn't as much going on in the home so there is time to walk and talk. Grandpa just might have time to sit and build a model or teach how to make a really good loaf of bread. This change of pace permits the discussion of values and traditions. It can be win–win with children bringing a distraction from the problems of later life and a reminder of the past and those that have moved on.

As with many lifelong learning experiences, it is not only the "doing" that teaches but the "being." Knowing that the extended family is always there instils a sense of roots, of stability; that the family is broad and supportive and that someone will be there even if mom or dad can't be. History starts to be lived right in the dining rooms of our world as parents become grandparents, kids become parents and grandchildren arrive. In time, we will be the grandparents and our children the parents and the world will spin on. Multi-generational family experiences teach this experience and can help to ground the world as it constantly changes.

For many families, though, this perfect scenario lives only in a storybook. The reasons are many: a grandparent is ill, physically or mentally; parenting styles differ and criticisms abound. The parent–grandparent relationship can be the source of many mixed emotions – guilt, jealousy, pride, disappointment – and it is sometimes easier to do without. It can be difficult to pinpoint exactly when or how these relationships fell apart, which can make them tricky to repair. The constant change can be the root of the problem. When we are in our own parents' house, it can be difficult to know how to be a parent to our children while we are still a child to our parents.

Lifelong patterns of behaviour don't change themselves without some thought and preparation. Yet even this discomfort in a relationship can serve as a valuable source of learning for ourselves and our children.

When grandparents feel differently about parenting choices or decisions being made, as parents it can help us to clarify our values and the reasons behind making different choices from those of our parents. Knowing the foundations of our decisions, we can practise assertiveness with our parents – respectfully stating our difference of opinion and asking for what we need. Our kids get to watch assertiveness and a respect for diversity in action. They learn from how we handle relationships, when we choose to persevere and when we decide to bow out of relationships that are detrimental to our own mental health.

If our parents are ill and require care, our children may end up involved in the day-to-day caring for their grandparents and the observation of all aspects of aging. They learn devotion, kindness, perseverance as parents continue to care for their own parents, giving back what they had been given. Being present as a grandparent ages and passes provides a child the first opportunities to learn about the circle of life and to being to understand the path of all living things.

The relationships that take place in multi-generational family can be rewarding or destructive, a bit of both or somewhere in between. As with most things in real life, they are rarely black and white but exist in various shades of gray. It can be difficult to have the real relationship turn out as something different than the dream, but even then we all have the opportunity to learn. We can grieve relationships that weren't or we can grieve relationships that were but that have passed on. Our kids gain the opportunity to see that all life is a mixture of pleasure and adversity and that the challenge is to learn how to live with both. We learn how to interact with our parents as adults rather than children and that we don't have to keep proving ourselves to our parents as was once the case. Finally, grandparents continue to learn these lessons along with us: the true lessons of life.

What else is going on?
Stop yelling at your kids

When we are coaching, a big part of what we hear from parents is that they find themselves yelling at their kids without being able to stop. When they look back at the situation, they can't figure out why they got so mad – in the light of day everything seems reasonable – most people don't expect their kids to be perfect. So how do things get so out of hand? There is usually something else going on.

Fear: You see your little guy running out into the street and a car is coming. You scream, "STOP" and everyone freezes. You grab your son, apologize to the driver and try to get back to normal. This is actually the best reason to lose it on your kid. Yelling is an effective parenting technique. We need it from time to time to keep our kids safe. If we yell all the time, it is a bit like crying wolf; the yelling is so commonplace that it doesn't even faze our kids. This is a great reason to get yelling under control so that we can use it when we really need it.

Repetition (Insanity): *I told you yesterday, and the day before, and for the last two months that this isn't allowed but you just did it again.* If the misbehaviour is so predictable that you could write a script for it, guess what? You already have.

Parent thinks: *Maybe today will be the day that she puts her stuff in the dishwasher... no she left it on the table yet again.*

Parent again (yelling): *WHEN WILL YOU LEARN?! WHY DO I ALWAYS HAVE TO TELL YOU TO PUT YOUR STUFF AWAY? CAN'T YOU DO IT ON YOUR OWN FOR A CHANGE?*

Daughter: *I won't do it again. I'm sorry okay! It's just some dishes.*

But really, it is not just about the dishes. It is about the fact that you have said it before and have had to say it again. You are being ignored. That is the reason for the yelling. Einstein defined insanity as doing the same thing over and over again and expecting different results. That is really what this second yelling reason is all about. If you want it to change, you need to do more than just hope it changes. You need to be the change. You need to change her routine so that she isn't allowed to get any farther than the dishwasher before she goes on to the next part of her day. There is no reason for our kids to change if we don't change ourselves.

Getting even with... Did your big brother pick on you every chance he got? Are you harder on your older child every time she trips her younger sib? Or maybe you are the one that always got in trouble when your younger sibling bugged you so much you just had to get back at her. If so, are you harder on your little one?

Sometimes, when we see our kids reliving things that happened to us, our emotions come into play. The discipline we dish out may be for our kids' misbehaviours combined with the need to get back at all older (or younger) siblings for what they did to us when we were young.

Hating that you used to... Do you still hate the fact that you can't keep your room clean? Is that why you are so hard on your child? Or maybe that little nagging fault that your daughter has is a characteristic of your spouse that you particularly detest. When you are yelling at your child, are you really yelling at your spouse or yourself?

Some outbursts leave us with a bit of homework. If the situation is creating a lot more emotion that it warrants, we need to make a plan for ourselves. How do we get rid of the extra baggage?

1. **Admit that we are carrying it.** The first step to making change is truly seeing what is there. Take a look at the situations that are causing the yelling and see if you can find any extra emotional baggage that is coming along for the ride. Once you recognize it, you can move to plan B.

2. **Drop it off somewhere else.** Rather than carrying the baggage around in your head, get it out of there. Talk about it or write it down so that you can face it head on. There is a good chance that the adult you are now has better skills to deal with the baggage than the kid you were when the problem was created. You don't have to solve everything before moving to plan C, but put it aside so that your logical brain can create a new script.

3. **Plan a new response.** We often yell when we don't know what else to say. When you are not in the moment, think about how you would like the situation to play out. Create something you can say that states what you want, in a respectful way. We can help you with this part and you will start to learn how to do it on your own.

4. **Work with our kids to give them new strategies.** Once you know what you are going to say – and do – to stop the habit from continuing, you need to let your kids know what is going to happen. *When you are done eating, the dishes go in the dishwasher. Let's practise that now – this is where you put your cup and the cutlery goes here. Before any of us leave the table, we will be sure that this step happens. What should we say if we see a snack dish left on the counter? How would you like us to give you one reminder? We could say, please finish with your dish. You will then stop what you are doing and put the dish away immediately. If this doesn't work, we will have to come up with a new plan to help remind you of your responsibilities.*

It isn't always easy. That's why we are here to help. Just like with our own children, there is often an emotion lurking behind our adult misbehaviours (yelling, treating our kids poorly). Just trying to change the misbehaviour without looking at the emotion is like putting a Batman Band-Aid on a gaping wound. Being aware of what else is going on is the first step to making this change.

Success at the Summer Fair!
Eliminating arguments before they start

If you are heading to a summer fair, here are some tips to stop parent–child arguments before they even get started.

What is there to fight about at a fair? You name it; we've seen families fighting about it. It doesn't have to be that way.

- **Plan first**
  Do a little planning before you head out. Decide what makes sense for your family and let your kids know the plan from the start; involve them in the planning if you can.

- **Junk food**
  One corn dog, the works or somewhere in between? Decide now so that your kids don't have to beg and you don't have to argue.

- **Money**
  What's your limit for spending? Are you paying for everything or will the kids need to use their allowance for games and souvenirs? This will make yes and no much easier in the heat of the moment.

- **Rides**
  How many are allowed? Which ones are off limits? Who is paying for them? How long are you willing to stand in line for that roller coaster anyway?

- **Home time**
  Let your kids know the time that you are leaving, give them warnings and then stick to what you say. If you know that you will cave when your kids beg you to stay, just decide to stay without setting the limit – match your words and your actions. If you know your kids will melt down at a certain time, GO HOME before then please.

- **Too rich for my blood**
  There are often good money-saving deals to be had on tickets to the fair but if a trip to the grounds is beyond your budget, choose other activities around the city that may be a fit. Rather than saying *We can't afford it*, which may leave your kids wondering if you can pay the next grocery bill, say, *We're choosing to spend our money differently this year.*

- **Teens on their own?**
  If you are worried about tweens/teens being at the fair on their own, go together and then set short times for them to go off and meet back at a prearranged space and time. This will help them to learn responsibility and you to determine whether they are ready for more freedom next year.

- **Safety**
  Talk through with your kids what they would do if they got lost. Don't just tell them what to do, be sure that they can tell you what they would do. They need to know (or have with them) contact info for you.

Have a safe and fun time at the fair!

Are we really helping?
Stop fixing things for kids

One evening at the lake, one of our sons discovered a large rock that weighed almost as much as he did. He decided that he wanted to move that rock down the beach and get it into the water. He experimented with pushing it, prying it, pulling it, lifting it – whatever he could do to get it closer to the water's edge. As parents, we sat back and watched – we were chatting about something and he seemed to be enjoying his activity.

A stranger sitting just down the beach from us wanted to help him and began offering bits of advice, *You should really come at it from this direction so you don't break your foot by dropping the rock on it.* The advice was taken and the boy went back to moving the rock, this time with his hands.

Again, the stranger commented, *Careful you don't break your fingers under the rock.* One of us responded, comically, *That's why God gave you ten digits... do your best to keep them all.* We didn't jump in to help him because he was working on it and learning and to the best of our assessment wasn't going to hurt himself because he had been around for his nine or so years of life and knew his way in the world.

Bit by bit, the rock got closer and closer to the water. There was a lot of experimentation happening and a lot of learning taking place. Now came the next step... how to get it into the water? One of us asked, *Is there anything on the beach that you could use to help you lift that rock? Anything you could use for a lever?*

Together, we found a stick (lever) and a rock to use as a fulcrum and experimented with how far out the fulcrum had to be to move the rock. We managed to get the rock up and over, right in the water.

As we were experimenting on the next step to get the rock deeper, the stranger came over and asked if he could help. He picked the rock up and tossed it, with some effort as it was quite heavy, into the water. The job was done. Wait, was it a job? The game was done.

So, a day later, we're using this example in an article because while the stranger obviously thought he was helping... we're not so sure that he was. You've often heard Parenting Power say, *When we do things for our kids that they can do for themselves, we are de-meaning them.*

But what about when it is something that they are motivated to discover for themselves even if they can't yet do it? What if the stranger hadn't stepped in? Would the boy have continued to problem solve? Would he have given up? Would he have asked for help? We don't really know the answer. He was pretty happy that his goal of getting the rock in the water was achieved.

From the outside looking in, we can't help but wonder what was better — the product (the rock in the water) or the process (getting it there)?

There probably isn't a real answer to this question. There's a good chance that the boy learned that strangers can be helpful, that we can rely on others when we need help...maybe he has forgotten all about it. It seemed to us to be a good parable: sometimes, when we think that we are helping others, we might be standing in the way of their learning. If we think they need help, we can ask them questions to help them find the answers they need. Our kids can't learn to solve their problems if we step in between them and the problem — at that point, they can't even see the problem...nor the many possible solutions.

AUGUST

The lazy hazy days of summer
Promoting independence as school begins

The end of August and the beginning of September always feel to us like the real New Year. This is when our kids' milestones are often most recognizable: starting preschool, headed to kindergarten, elementary school or beyond. The summer has been filled with moments of doing absolutely nothing – lazy, lazy, lazy.

It's hazy that will get the bulk of the focus in this article. That's because whenever new beginnings come around, it's a great time to check whether our vision of our children is a little hazy. As we start to get them ready for whatever is around the corner, we need to be sure that we are seeing them for who they truly are and not who they were a few months ago before summer started.

It would be easy for us as parents to fall right back into last year's habits – especially those of us with school-aged children. We could keep the old routines and pick up where we left off. BUT – that might land us in a place where we are doing more for our kids than we need to be. Whenever we "over" do for our children, we are demeaning them; literally taking away some of their meaning – their sense of self. Few parents set out to do this but many fall into that hazy-viewed trap.

Here are some tips to help you see your children clearly as they grow:

1. Make a mental list of the tasks you currently do for your child.

2. Pick five that your child could master developmentally now that couldn't have happened the last time you checked.

3. Plan with your kids for them to learn some of these new tasks. This often works well if you first do the tasks with your child and then transition to them doing the tasks on their own.

You'll find a list of age-appropriate tasks on our website in case you need some ideas.

Enjoy the end of summer and the new-found freedom that comes as our children grow a greater sense of self.

How did I end up with that kid?
Setting clear expectations

How does it happen?

My child just won't pick up her toys.

My son will not practise the piano.

I'm not sure how I got the kid who doesn't do homework.

Lately, there seems to be a sense of exasperation in the voices of parents we meet. They can't seem to understand how they got the child with a specific misbehaviour. It's as if this behaviour was handed to the infant just prior to the stork gathering up the bundle and dropping it in the cabbage patch for the parents to discover.

There is no question that temperament plays a factor in every human. Statistically, one in four children will be a pleaser, two in four will go along with some motivation and the last one will fight things tooth and nail. If you happen to be blessed with a child in the latter category, it is going to take a great deal more structure and consistency to get through to that one. That's what we call parenting.

At Parenting Power we believe that KIDS ARE CAPABLE. They are capable of so much, they are capable of meeting our expectations and they are capable of learning from their parents. If parents declare the fact, *My daughter will not pick up her toys,* they are correct. She will believe them. She will live that declaration passionately.

Parenting is about taking responsibility to expect our kids to be capable of learning and to encourage them with words and actions that say, *I know you can do this. I know you can learn and I'm here to teach you.*

For many kids, it is not until we expect them to practise piano, pick up toys and/or do homework that it will happen. Then we need to work with our kids to develop a plan for that to happen. If your child knows that all she has to do is create a big fuss about doing homework, or ignore it and put up with your ranting or your own ignoring of the behaviour in order to get out of it, you have taught her well. NOW you need to take the time to teach the right way for homework to happen (or clean up, or piano, or dishes or whatever it is in your house).

How does it happen? How did you get that kid? Well, we all get the kids we get. What happens next is up to us. We need to practise awareness and see what is happening – what we like and what we don't like. Then, we need to figure out how to change what we don't like.

We can choose to play the role of victim and claim that we just got the kid who won't clean up. Or we can take responsibility for the situation and make a plan to teach our child how to clean up: What are the expectations, the consequences? How will we teach this task? What amount of time do we need to work on this with our child? How do we schedule that?

This is real-life parenting – communicating clearly, acknowledging feelings and using language that encourages our kids to do what needs to happen in real life. They don't have to like loading and unloading the dishwasher. They need to know that complaining about it won't make the task go away. Doing the task is what makes it go away...until tomorrow.

That's how it happens! Need some help? We're here.

When your best friend doesn't parent like you
Surviving relationship challenges

Think back to those first few months of pregnancy. Everything was a mixture of excitement and trepidation. Every day brought new feelings and dreams of what life would be like as a young family. News of friends or family who were also pregnant launched visions of walking together with strollers, relaxing play dates in which the children would enjoy each other and you could too. Even now, when we meet an old friend who has children the same age as our own, the ideas start flowing: *Let's head to the beach this weekend! Come out and join us at the cottage for a week.*

Thankfully, things often do work out just right between friends and their children. But what happens when things head in the other direction?

End-of-summer conversations bring news of summer vacations gone wrong: children who fought like cats and dogs, parents who could not believe the way their friends parented. One parent mentioned that she felt like a complete failure because her children did not get on well with the children of an old friend as they vacationed together. *Does this happen to other parents too?* she asked.

Of course, this happens to many of us. And even though summer is just about over, it is worth considering because these uncomfortable interactions occur during play dates, dinner parties, holiday meals, even on the school yard. They happen in every season and with children of different ages. Knowing that this is a pretty normal situation leads us to look at some strategies parents can use to get things working as well as they possibly can.

When you don't like the way your friend speaks to your child
This can be tricky – you didn't think your son misbehaved badly but your friend just tore a strip off him and favoured her son in the argument.

If it is really bad in the moment, speak to your son as you pull him aside, *I think that you and I need to talk about what just happened here and leave* [friend and her child] *to discuss it as a family.* Once you have your child out of harm's way, you can talk with him about the situation and parent in your way. When you are all together again, agree to specific rules for the activities that follow and include consequences, make sure everyone involved has heard them.

When your parenting styles are the same but your kids will not get along
Make sure that you are being realistic. If the kids have never met or are different ages and have little in common, create opportunities for parents and kids to do an activity to get to know each other. Plan some things that the children can do together and check in to see how things are going. Talk with the other parents to come up with a plan to handle disagreements among the children.

When you disagree about parenting AND your kids don't get along
Even though you dreamed of great times together, sometimes it is more trouble than it is worth. This doesn't mean that you never see these people. It does mean that you may choose to get a sitter and join these old friends for an adult dinner or getaway.

Just to be clear: there are many times in life in which our kids won't like another child or we don't like the way an adult handles a situation. Life is like that and learning to deal with it is a life skill. Many of the above examples are great opportunities for learning when you find yourself in them. However, when you have limited down-time and want to return from your vacation feeling relaxed with great memories, you don't have to choose to put yourself in the same situation repeatedly in the hopes that things will work out better next time.

Thankfully, there are other great summer vacation stories filling the days of September. Many are of new-found adult friendships with parents of our children's school friends. With a little luck and some great strategies, some of these new friendships may become the long-lasting, trouble-free relationships we dreamed about in our early parenting days.

There's a lot to be said for "nothing"
Allowing children to "do it themselves"

There are certain books that evoke a warm hug whenever one sees the cover page. Without even opening the book, you can recite pages of the text and see the pictures come alive, remembering countless readings and repetition with your young children even before they could talk. These are precious memories: the rhythmic lilt of the words, a special word here and there that your toddler would memorize and hold in a warm mouth waiting for the time to say it in the familiar place; your child's favourite picture that would be outlined with a tiny finger every time that page arrived.

One of those books is *Something from Nothing* by Phoebe Gilman. Many things about that book touch children's imagination and resonate with adults as well. In the story, the boy starts out with a favourite coat that eventually is too old to wear but Grandpa the tailor makes it into a vest and then a tie and keeps making something wonderfully new from something old and worn out.

This same title seemed really appropriate for one of the guiding philosophies of Parenting Power. The idea that there are many times in parenting where the best thing we can do for our kids is "nothing." What do we mean by that? Well, in our culture, there seems to be a prevailing feeling that the more we can do for our kids, the better things will be for them. We don't want them to struggle, so we handle their problems. We don't want them to suffer so we make their lunches, pack their school bags, finish their homework, fight their battles. It seems like a good idea at the time – why wouldn't we help our kids? The reason is because when we do for our kids what they can do for themselves, we are literally de-meaning them... we are taking away their meaning or sense of purpose.

Often, our words tell our children, *You can do anything*! and at the same time, our actions tell them – *you need me to do that for you*. It is faster, often neater and easier for us to jump in and do things for our kids – but they are not learning how to do it for themselves. Doing everything for our kids means that we are often exhausted and that our kids expect things to be done for them.

So, do we put the kids out on the sidewalk with a suitcase, a loaf of bread and a jar of peanut butter and let them fend completely for themselves? If you have spent time with Parenting Power, you'll know that we believe in Taking Time to Teach. Whenever we want our kids to take on new experiences, we set them up for success. We show them what needs to be done, invite their suggestions, do it with them and then watch them do it on their own.

As we back away, they are learning to manage things for themselves; one task at a time. When we step back and do nothing, they are getting something from that nothing:

- The feeling that comes from learning how to do something new

- A greater sense of self and their abilities

- The knowledge that what seemed too hard before is now easier through perseverance

- The confidence that we believe they are capable of tackling this new skill

- The courage to try another new thing

Every family will find ways to share or delegate tasks to their kids and in doing so, the children will see how families work together sharing both the responsibilities and the privileges that come from living in a supportive community.

When we allow kids to do for themselves, they gain so much and, with their newly learned strengths, they can help someone who needs their help, increasing interdependence and eventually give the gift of something from nothing to someone else.

Get your kids ready for back to school
Five ways to make your life easier

They're heading back and now's the time to get them ready. Whether it is their first day ever or just the first day for this grade, here are five things to consider.

1. **Take a good look at your kid** A lot has changed since last June and definitely since last September. Check and see what your child can do independently. Do you really need to help her pack up her backpack (no) or get his lunchbox ready (maybe)? When we do for our kids what they could do for themselves, we are demeaning them: taking away their meaning. Our actions tell them that they can't do it on their own and decreases their sense of self.

2. **Unload your plate** What will you require your child to do this year? Will your daughter get her own breakfast ready? Will your son make his lunch or sweep the kitchen floor while you finish off the lunches? Get an idea of one or two chores that your child will take off your plate. Ultimately, this will leave you feeling less stressed and a bit more patient.

3. **Take time to teach** Now that you know what to hand off to your kids, take the time to teach it. Break the chore down into smaller tasks, create a check list if necessary and work with them as they begin to feel more capable. Don't load them down with tons of new chores — just one or two. That way, you'll be setting them up for

success. Start now so that they can practise when there is no school and feel capable when they head back.

4. **Sleep matters** Check out how much sleep your child needs and find a way to make that happen. Sleep affects our bodies and our brains. Making it a priority will be a great gift to your child as well as an important habit.

5. **Routines help** Whether it is getting out the door, getting to dance class, getting homework done or getting kids to sleep, creating a routine with your child will make things easier on everyone. Ask your youngster to help you make a list of the tasks required (getting to dance class: fill water bottle, pack bag with shoes and water bottle, change into gear). Write down an order, how long each thing will take, as well as who is responsible for each task (get the child helping as much as possible). Decide on how you will cue tasks and what the consequences are for following plan and not following plan. Knowing all of this will help to keep everyone calm in the heat of the moment.

Get your kids ready for a healthy school year that will help them and you!

SEPTEMBER

Balance
Living your values

Balance is a tough word – even saying it can stress us out. We hear it on the radio and TV and see it on magazine covers (mostly women's magazines) every week. For us (Gail and Julie) it immediately brings to mind a woman trying to juggle way too many breakable objects (vases, plates, crystal goblets…flaming torches) and praying that none of them drop. This individual is working so hard to keep everything safe that the thing most likely to fall to pieces is the juggler herself. That is why we don't really like to use the word balance anymore. We got tired of worrying about breaking things…because anyone who is a mom knows that things are going to get broken.

Knowing the power of words, we decided to stop using the word "balance" and have begun looking for another word. One that we heard recently is "harmony." To us, harmony means "things co-existing and not all items being in the air at the same time, nor having equal weight on either sides of the teeter-totter." This word seems more peaceful and lets us off the hook a bit. And in general, that may be what we were striving for with that other word anyway.

At Parenting Power we believe that every family is unique (our two families certainly are). No one person's definition of harmony or the "B word" will work for everyone. Some of us get in a rut when we have nothing on our schedule and like to have a variety of things to keep us busy. Others get flustered when there is more than one thing that needs to happen at any one time, which seems to be a constant when children enter the picture.

We have the privilege of talking with many parents, all trying to do the best job possible. Those with infants tell us that they can't find the time to sleep, read, exercise or be with their spouses. Those with toddlers tell us that they loved having the opportunity to be able to carry the infants in car seats to wherever they needed to go, but that they feel limited by their children having to nap all the time so they can't get out and get things done. Those with preschool-aged children tell us that they miss their children's nap time so much because it allowed them time to read or rest and that it is overwhelming to have the children around so much, always busy and into things. Those with school-aged children tell us that they miss having the children around during the day and then become harried with all of the driving after school to lessons of every kind.

The busyness and juggling seem to stay with us and it is very easy to get caught up in how the balance of the past does not fit into our current situation. It never will. However, the time spent grieving that loss or, worse yet, trying to retrieve the past is being modelled to our children. And therein lies the problem.

PARENTING WITH A PLAN

We believe in Parenting with a Plan. The plan begins by looking at what is really important to you and your family. This may differ from what is important to your neighbours. There is often a tendency to get caught up in the values and goals of those around us. Comparing ourselves to our peers is a natural process; however, we must strive to use these comparisons as a way of reaffirming our own needs, desires, goals and visions.

Harmony is about figuring out where you are and how you feel about being there. Sometimes it's finding satisfaction in being at that point. Sometimes it is about realizing that this part of your life is tough and that it will be that way for the next piece of time. But that is just the starting point. Here is where the plan part comes in.

When you know what values are important to your family (for example, patience, solitude, independence, compassion, kindness) you can begin to visualize how you currently live these values and model them to your children. We model values by living them. Here are some steps to help you in your plan.

1. **Focus on what you are doing**, not what you are failing to accomplish. If you need to, write down how many diapers you change, how many meals you are making, how many gifts you are giving to your family and yourself through your daily efforts. Sometimes, just seeing what you are achieving helps you to feel better about your current situation.

2. **If you are not finding time for yourself on a regular basis, make it**. If you can, do it in front of your children in order to model for them the need for quiet time and regeneration. This will look different as your kids grow. Initially it may be with them rocking in a baby swing, later on – bouncing in the excer-saucer. Getting out for a run may mean putting your child in the stroller and heading out for some alone time together. Perhaps it is reading by the pool during swimming lessons at some point. It can also be when your little ones practise their quiet time or independent play. We need to model for our children that being alone with ourselves doesn't equate with being lonely.

3. **Hold on to who you are**. When we become moms, some of us take on that role so whole-heartedly that we neglect every other potential role (independent woman, thinker, reader, healthy/vibrant being, lover of travel, gardener, welder, you-name-it). Once we become "The Mom," it can be really difficult to allow our children to grow up and become more independent because we will then have no role to fill. Achieving harmony means letting our children do more of what they can do for themselves and flexing these other roles every once in a while, on our own or with our children.

By encouraging our children's independence through modelling our own acceptance of our situation and who we are or want to be, we walk ever closer to living harmony.

Firm or soft?
Setting limits

In the aftershock of childbirth, we spend our days just trying to get by. Sleep is a remnant of the distant past. Life as we knew it ceases – or at least retreats. We begin anew, learning how to function with this new being who depends on us for every need. As the months progress, we start to get the hang of it and many of us feel as if we are coasting for a while until the time when our little one suddenly hits *that* point. You know what we are talking about…the day little Sweet-Cheeks says "NO!" It usually happens around 18 months, sometimes even before then.

At Parenting Power this is what sets our phone ringing much of the time: *Hi, I'm calling because my child is 18 months and my world is crumbling!*

We hear that a lot and that's okay! Because that is the point at which, if you haven't been doing it already, you need to be Parenting with a Plan. As parents, this is the first time that we are really being asked about the way things work, sometimes by children who only have three or four words. They can ask pretty loudly though, so here are some thoughts on getting you through from 18 months until they leave home.

Children are not born with knowledge of right and wrong. Sometimes we expect babies to know social norms and values, but they don't. What we see as misbehaviour is just their curiosity and exploring. As they grow older and gain more knowledge of the world, they begin to test what they believe to be true.

Kids test because they want to know what the limits are. We all want to know the limits in our daily lives. If we know the structure, we can predict what will happen in our day and we feel more comfortable about it. Speed limits, bus schedules, job descriptions – these are just some of the limits set out for us as adults each and every day.

Children are little scientists, collecting data on how the world works each moment of the day. Once they have the data, they test it – *Yesterday this made mom look at me but today it didn't, what will happen now if I do it louder?* The minute we respond differently, they test again.

So our reaction to our children's behaviour plays a very large role in the behaviour itself, as does our ability to set out the boundaries or limits in advance. Taking the time to teach our children is a gift that lasts a lifetime.

Many people think that they are setting clear limits for their children. They don't understand why there is miscommunication. Often the limits being set by parents are soft limits – the yellow light of limits. When we are driving down the street and see a green light, we know that the signal means GO. A red traffic light means only one thing, STOP. But the yellow light is in a league of its own. It can mean *Slow down, Speed up*, or *Take a risk and gun it for all it's worth.* The decision of what to do is ultimately left in the hands of the driver. If the driver is two years old, clear communication flies out the window.

Here are examples of some of our favourite soft limits heard regularly across the nation.

The Question
Dad: *It's time to have a bath, okay?*

Child: *No Dad, it's not okay. Thanks for asking.*

Mom: *Are you ready for bed sweetie?*

Child: *No Mom, I want to keep playing.*

The Plead
Mom: *Honey, I really wish you wouldn't run when you have food in your mouth.*

Mom: *Honey, you shouldn't hit your brother like that.*

Child's thought: *Thanks for telling me how you feel mom. I think I'll do it a few more times though because you let me.*

Of course there are many more examples but our space here is limited. Sometimes it isn't even our words that send soft limits, it is our actions.

When we tell our child that he is capable of going to the bathroom in the toilet and then we put him in pull-up diapers "just in case," we are really saying: *We know that you won't be able to do it so we are getting you to wear this diaper – go ahead and use it instead of the potty.*

Take a look at the messages you are sending to your child and be sure that you are saying things clearly. Take the questions (*okay?*) out of your instructions at times when there is no choice. Use sentence starters like:

- *I expect you to…* [go upstairs and have a bath]

- *The clock says it is time to…* [get in the car and head to school]

- *When … we…* [when we eat, we stay still]

As parents we need to pick our battles. If we limit everything, then our children will balk. They really do need to feel like they have some freedom and choice in the matter. Limits also have to change with age and ability. Children derive a greater sense of involvement if there are choices within limits. *Would you like to go to bed at 7:30 or 7:35? You decide.*

STRATEGIES FOR A CLEARER FORM OF COMMUNICATION

- Decide what your family values are regarding the issue at hand — these may be different from those of your neighbour or your child's best friend. That's okay.

- Let these values guide what the boundaries or limits of the situation will be.

- Write out the rule or the limit so that you are sure that it is a firm limit (a red or green light).

- Share these limits with your children so that they have a clear understanding of the expectations. You may want to make a poster of the rules (with pictures if your little one can't yet read) so that everyone can remember the expectations.

- Make a commitment not to be the second player in a power struggle. If your strong-willed child will not let go of a point, close your mouth and walk away until she can speak to you in a calm voice.

Of course the age of your child will have an impact in this process but it is worth starting it early. By the age of one, most children understand 80 per cent of what we are saying. This doesn't mean that they are fully in control of their bodies and emotions — they will need our help to follow the limits. As children age, this help may change. We can tell them what *to do* rather than what *not to do*. When they are capable, involve children in the limit-setting process.

Ultimately, the ball is in our court. Our children are depending on us to show them what is expected, to meet them where they are and to set them up for success through teaching and discipline. We cannot walk on eggshells around our children. They need us to show them the way. We can only control our own behaviour, so let's plan how to express our limits and how to respond. When we pick our battles and model respectful communication, we feel confident about what we are doing, capable as parents and calm in our family interactions.

20:20 hindsight
Coping with daily struggles

No matter the age of your children, there is a good chance that at some point during their lifetime, you were filled with fear that the troubling behaviour of that moment would never cease and that you wouldn't be able to handle it for much longer. Whether it was in those first few weeks of life when you thought you might never sleep again, or when your four-month-old infant wouldn't nap and you wondered how you would ever have any time to yourself. Perhaps it was at two years of age when your child began to scream and hit and you questioned whether you had a future bully on your hands. Maybe it was at four years of age when your son reverted to peeing his pants and you feared being chained to the laundry room for the rest of your life. What about the year that your child printed illegibly, didn't listen in class or could not get the homework to come home from school or back to the teacher?

Maybe you've hit all of these milestones and more. Perhaps some of them lie ahead. The one commonality is the fact that, having passed them, we realise that they are now over. At the moment of crisis, it seemed like things would never change. It was easy to be dragged down by the fear that you were failing your child and that you would be doomed to fail them eternally because you could not see a way to change. And yet, here we are and, somehow, the change took place.

Our kids are supposed to misbehave and face challenges. Each of these situations is an opportunity for us to share new strategies and boundaries with our children. But let us take it one step further: each of these situations is also an opportunity for us as parents. We learn new parenting strategies, and in looking back, we can learn to have faith in the coming changes and to model this faith.

In generations past, and in some parts of the world even today, parents were so busy getting food to the table and focussing on keeping their children healthy and alive that the worry about not using the right parenting technique, or failing their children through missed opportunity, just didn't exist. For many of us now, there is a luxury of time to worry about every possible hardship that will come to our children; real and imagined:

- *Should they have already started violin lessons?*

- *Will they make it to the tier one team so that they are one step closer to the NHL?*

- *Do they know all of their times tables?*

- *Can they plan ahead and keep their rooms clean?*

It is wonderful to dream big dreams for our children, more wonderful still to support their own dreams. But as we take the steps that make up our day-to-day path, let us model hope, faith and trust that whatever difficulties we face (and they will come) we will find the strength, perseverance, courage and strategies to learn from them; that change will come and the struggle will result in greater resilience for us and our children.

We must also keep in mind that change happens as a process. Each day we are one day further in the process of teaching/learning a new behaviour or strategy. In real life, nothing happens in an instant – the troubles of the world do not instantly solve themselves in 30 minutes as it happens on TV. Parenting is a process; there will be moments when we can celebrate a specific product but we will derive the greatest pleasures from the day-to-day experiences while we are with our growing children. When we look back with hindsight, we'll know that some of the hardest times led to the birth of our greatest achievements and they were worth it.

Feeding wolves
Using positive scripts

*A Cherokee elder told his grandson: My son, there is a battle between two wolves inside us all. One is **Evil**. It is anger, jealousy, greed, resentment, inferiority, lies and ego. The other is **Good**. It is joy, peace, love, hope, humility, kindness, empathy and truth.*

The boy thought about it, and asked: Grandfather, which wolf wins?

The old man quietly replied: The one you feed.

Which wolf did you feed today? This saying has been around for many years and came to our attention again recently. It reminded us of the human fondness for habits. Repetition and routine gives us comfort even if it does not serve us in other ways. Our kids feel the same way.

At Parenting Power we talk about Family Habits. Your family might have a successful bedtime routine (bath, books, bed) or a swimming pool habit that really works (boy and dad go into one change room, girl and mom go into the other, set a time that everyone's out of the pool and head home — no arguments).

The ingredients of a successful family habit are:

- A clear understanding of the expectations and consequences by the parents

- Clear and simple communication of these expectations and consequences to the children

- Taking the time to teach the process the way we want it to work

- Following through with consequences

Families also develop challenging family habits: nagging and yelling when getting ready in the morning; fights about homework or mealtimes; struggles at bedtime or kids getting out of bed throughout the evening and through the night.

The ingredients of a challenging family habit are:

- Being uncertain as parents about exactly what's expected

- Giving kids the benefit of the doubt with excuses (she's tired, he's hungry, it's been a long day)

- Changing what we tell the children about expectations – lots of exceptions to the rules if there even are rules

- Lots of talking, nagging, whining, blaming, shaming by parents

- Lack of consequences being assigned

- Lack of follow through with consequences

- HOPING THAT IT WILL GO BETTER TOMORROW

Einstein's definition of insanity was "Doing the same thing over and over again and expecting different results." We agree.

A family was telling us about a child who does not like daycare at all right now – it is much less stimulating than the child's school experiences. Every evening before daycare, she starts to complain about having to go. In the morning, she is tense and anxious. The whole family is just waiting for the tantrum to begin. It usually does when dad is getting out of the car to take her into daycare. She screams, cries, holds onto him, begs – it is a huge scene every time. Mom and dad continue to tell her that she knows that she'll be fine at daycare, that she is going there whether she screams or not. They reassure her that she can do it; they get frustrated and angry and eventually leave with everyone feeling horrible. They do this all in the moment...every time. Yuck!

Walking away from the child at that moment, we begin to feed the wolf: *She's driving me crazy! I hate that she does that! Why can't she see that she is fine?! When will she learn that it will be okay?! It must be something I'm doing wrong! What's wrong with me?! Why can't I make it stop?! Other people don't have this problem! What's wrong with me? What's wrong with her?*

Sounds like a full meal for the wolf who continues to munch on the left-overs for the rest of the day. So how do we change it?

- We have to know that we are in the habit. When we have created a gourmet meal for the evil wolf, we know we are there!

- We need to know how we want it to look.

- Once we know, we need to set it up for the child that things are going to be different. We do this in a calm time and place. We talk about the new words that she will say, and the new ways that we will respond to her behaviour.

Changing a habit means that we have to script our response so that there is a change. Rather than being dragged into the dance, we can choose to step off the dance floor.

FEEDING THE RIGHT WOLF

Somewhere in this process, we have to begin to feed the other wolf: the good one. When things aren't working, it is easy to get dragged down into the negative spiral. It may feel like we have no choice.

We have a choice every time. If you really need to feed that big, bad wolf, set a timer and feed it for the full time on the clock. Then, see how you might feed his brother.

When we pull ourselves out of the emotional turmoil, we can begin to see the other person's side (in this case, the child). Just because we understand their perspective, doesn't mean we have to agree with it. Once we allow ourselves to see that the other side exists, we can remind ourselves of the commonalities shared between us and the other person. From there, we can have compassion. We can realise that it is likely not the child we dislike, but the situation and the behaviour. Can we work together against the situation? That puts us both on the same side.

The discussion shifts from *What's wrong with you? Why won't you accept it the way it is?* to *How do we make this situation better together?*

Suddenly, we are feeding the other wolf.

There is no question that our kids spend time feeding these wolves as well. So how do we make them change? We can't. We can't change anyone else's behaviour.

What we can do is teach strategies. We know that kids live what they learn and learn what they live so the most effective way to teach is to model. Talk about the Cherokee legend. Talk about feeding the wolves and realising that you were doing it. When we share our awareness, our strengths and our weaknesses, we begin to help others do the same.

Wishing you many wonderful wolf meals!

OCTOBER

Getting ready for Thanksgiving dinner
Teaching table manners

Parents have been struggling to teach their children table manners for many years. Even back in 1530, Erasmus in his Treatise on Manners advised, "Be careful not to be the first to put your hands in the dish. What you cannot hold in your hands you must put on your plate. Also it is a great breach of etiquette when your fingers are dirty and greasy, to bring them to your mouth in order to lick them, or to clean them on your jacket. It would be more decent to use the tablecloth."

With Thanksgiving dinner around the corner and other holiday meals not far behind, it might be nice to have lived in the 1500s. Many young children today would be (and actually have been) delighted to use the tablecloth to wipe their hands, often with a few dishes and a drink or two landing in their laps.

Formal family meals can strike fear or at least angst in the hearts of parents everywhere. On these occasions, with the in-laws visiting from out of town, it would be so nice for the children to sit with the adults at the table and act in a polite fashion. A common set of questions asked of Parenting Power during the holiday season include *How do I keep my daughter seated at the table? What can I do to keep my son from spitting Grandma's Brussels sprouts onto the table?*

While we are not born with manners and certainly don't gain them by osmosis, we do learn them from those around us. Deciding upon the etiquette that is important to your family is a great place to start. Clarifying and teaching it to the children comes next. With this preparation, you can decrease some of the spills and embarrassment at the dinner table, leaving time to be genuinely thankful that everyone has come together for the meal.

Here are some of Parenting Power's suggestions to get you to that point.

Model manners that you would like your children to adopt
- Leaving forks on the table when not eating with them

- Thanking the chef for the food

- Keeping the *Yuck*, *Gross* and *I hate that* comments in your head

- Learning how to have one taste and then say, *No thank you.*

Explain your expectations to the children and teach them ahead of time
A fun way to do this is by having some practise sessions of pretend dinners and tea parties.

Keep your expectations realistic
Children under two years of age probably won't stay at the table for a long time after eating without causing quite a fuss. Older children can be expected to stay longer and can wait for their same-age peers to finish.

Involve the children in the dinner conversation
It is pretty boring when all the talk is about finance and gossip when all you know is that Hot Wheels cost $1.69 and that Suzy got moved for talking in class today.

Involve the children in the preparation
Setting the table, making place cards or even preparing a portion of the dinner are all activities that can help the child to participate in and anticipate the special qualities of the meal.

Table manners may vary depending on the table – kitchen table, Grandma's dining room or fancy restaurant. This is okay. What does need to remain consistent is the manner in which you express your expectations and follow through. Manners are learned over time but it is never too early to start. Here's to many happy family meals!

Be the change
Modelling your values

You must be the change you want to see in the world. —Mahatma Ghandi

During these times of lengthening darkness and festive celebration, there is a tendency to cling to ritual and tradition; remembering previous holidays with family, hoping to recapture that childlike feeling of wonder at the sparkle of lights, the delightful anticipation of a special goodie, favourite meal, exciting gift or treasured story. Stopping to think about those moments-gone-by can bring the feeling right back – a rush of the heart, a smile, a crinkle around the eyes. Those joys are a wonder to recall.

In all likelihood, the memories came about at a time when we were not knee-deep in planning "just the right gift" or the best menu for the season, or figuring out how to get everything done in the few days left. We were present, open to experiencing whatever new thing was placed before us and excited about the wonders that were certain to arrive.

We were open to change because we didn't know what to expect. Now, as adults, it is sometimes hard to remember that the only thing we know to expect is CHANGE. We can never re-create those memories of our childhood exactly and our children shed a special new light on our old traditions. It is striking how much energy we put into fighting against the certainty of change. If we work harder or longer or spend more money, we can just hold onto what we know for sure. All that effort can be exhausting.

Change is often tough precisely because of the uncertainty. Parenting Power talks regularly about the comfort of routine and predictability for our kids; those routines provide some stability to weather the changes that arise. Many adults treasure routine for the same reason. It's great to live feeling comfortable with a sense of how things will happen. The danger is to become so attached to the plan that when it shifts (and it's going to shift), we can't cope.

As this year winds down and another year begins, here are two ideas to consider:

- We can remind children that change happens to everyone (not because they are bad) and we can support our kids in learning to weather change by giving them the opportunity to make choices and experience the consequences of their choices – as we all need to do when change comes along.

- We can support ourselves in the hours, days, weeks and years ahead by accepting that change is coming and by *being* the change.

That's right – if there is a character trait that you would like to see developing in your children this year, *be* it. If generosity and gratitude is what you wish for them, live it out loud. Practise it daily, mention it regularly – not in nagging them to do it, but in showing them that you are living it. Kids live what they learn. Practise the change and invite your kids to take part. When we are the change we want to see in the world, our kids see it and learn it and live it and become the change themselves.

When do children stop fighting for power?
Solving power struggles

It starts as a toddler. Our little one refuses to hand over a toy or stop an activity. In his mind, the idea that anyone would want to stop him from doing what he is doing is inconceivable due to his egocentric stage of development. There is only one point of view — his own. HOW could mom or dad want something different than what he knows to be true for his happiness?

It continues through ages three and four. Egocentric development gives way and our preschooler starts to realise that there are other points of view. But she is often being told what to do, and where/when to do it. As she realises that she is more capable, she fights for the opportunity to control the situation.

Does it stop in kindergarten? Elementary school? Certainly not junior high, and kids are pushing for control through high school and beyond.

What about at work? On the hockey rink? Wouldn't it be great to finally have control on the golf course? What about if those other drivers would learn how to drive the right way — like us? How about when our kids don't listen or do what we want them to do?

Wait a minute? Do we ever stop fighting for control? That, Dear Reader, is up to you.

Humans love predictability. We crave routine and love to know how things are going to happen with all of the details. We often dread change and will work hard to preserve the status quo even when we don't really like it that much. And yet it has been said that the only two constants in the world are death and taxes. Taxes are always changing and death is something of a change itself. Change is all we have going for us and controlling it is pretty hard to do.

This explains our love of routine – it brings us safety and predictability and a false sense of control in a world where things are constantly in flux. When we think about it that way, it is not hard to see why our kids want control/ power from such an early age. Knowing how things are going to work brings comfort, a sense of safety and intelligence.

So how do we stop the fight for control?

1. **Stop fighting.** It takes two to tango – if one of us stops, the dance is over. Often when facing a defiant child, it is easy to get caught up in the race to be the one with more power. *I'm the adult, I'm the parent, what I say goes!* We are modelling the fight for power and our kids learn this one quite well. At Parenting Power we rely on a change in perception: "You against your child" becomes "You <u>and</u> your child" against the situation. Suddenly, you and your child are on the same side, working together to solve the problem. You might say, *Wow – we have a problem here. I want this and you want this, how are we going to make this happen?*

2. **Hand over power when it can be handed over.** There are many situations in which parents must have the final say. However, in many instances, we are maintaining power in situations where it is no longer required and doing things for our children that they are able to do for themselves. Children's abilities are changing constantly and sometimes we are so busy with life that we don't see how capable they are. We argue with them about eating a snack, getting ready for school or doing homework when they are ready to be involved in

making a plan and doing it for themselves. It doesn't mean that we aren't there to love them, teach them and support them, but we can become open to their strengths and hand over some of the decision making and problem solving to them.

Ultimately, our ability to control what is happening in our lives is minimal and that can be very difficult to accept. Perhaps that is why we struggle to control the things we think we can: the behaviour of our children. Having realistic expectations of ourselves and the extent of our control can be the first step of awareness to giving up the fight. Modelling that for our children, may be the next.

A child who dreams
Allowing children to dream

Chances are, when your little bundle of joy made his or her way into the world, your heart was wide open and your head filled with dreams of what might be. Maybe it started even earlier; within moments of being told that they are pregnant, many parents begin to dream big dreams for the future.

Dreams are wonderful things. They help us to see past difficulties and uncertainty and they provide hope and direction for the future. They are the first steps to building changes into our lives, helping us to realise values and direction that guide us in our daily steps through life.

One of the most valuable qualities of dreams is their ethereal nature. Dreams are not concrete plans, they are abstract ideas and visions of what we hope will follow. It is this abstract quality that gives them the ability to float above us, like an abandoned helium balloon, the colourful globe pulling us forward and raising our spirits and our vision up toward what will be.

Unfortunately, transforming dreams to reality sometimes results in air being leaked out of the balloon. Capturing dreams and fitting them into our mould for how they will happen can squeeze out the ethereal nature or at least deflate the magic qualities of the initial dream.

This can happen daily as we raise our children. We started out with dreams of them being punctual, organized, polite, academically successful, healthy, fit, strong team players, great readers, able musicians, the list goes on... Now here we are having lived parts of our lives and knowing exactly how we think they can get to the place of our dreams and they don't even listen. We could save them so much trouble and strife, if only... But they don't.

Children teach us so many valuable lessons. They reflect our ugly sides and our great qualities. They take us to emotions we may never have reached without them; sometimes emotions that we never really wanted to feel in the first place. One of the greatest lessons we can learn from our children is about dreams.

We can want, wish, dream for something so badly and even know how we think it should happen. Sometimes wanting it so badly actually blinds us from getting there.

The lesson: While the dream can guide the way and open the door for things to happen, we need to stand back and allow it to happen at its own pace. Our children need to be involved in seeing the dream, wanting the dream and learning how to make it happen for it to be a valuable experience for them. It is the slow process of achieving the dream that adds to its value.

The second lesson: While our dreams might have been great for our children, they have their own dreams as well. They have mountains to climb or goals to reach that might seem entirely foreign to us. We can support them and join them in building the steps to achieving their own dreams. We can also teach them to make space to allow those dreams to happen at their own pace; that we don't have complete control and sometimes being patient will bring those dreams closer.

Supporting our kids in their dreams means asking them how they can solve problems, how they see the changes taking place. When we ask them, we show them that we believe that they are capable of solving problems. Not every suggestion will be a winner but trying those ones and learning from the mistakes will also help our children to learn. Ultimately, when we support our children in solving their own problems and in realizing their dreams, we will get what we really wanted when we first dreamed those dreams so long ago: healthy, independent, confident kids who become adults willing to try and fail and learn from those experiences and to try again as they strive for their own dreams.

NOVEMBER

Homework – How to make the most of it!
Stopping homework battles

By November, having met the new teachers and sharpened the new pencils, many of us are settling into the reality of the school year. As with many things, the reality is not always pretty. Agendas remind us that there is homework even though there may not be time for it to happen.

If you are a hardened homework parent, you may be reflecting on the homework battles and frustrations from last year, hesitant to jump into it again. One of the most common questions we answer is, "Why do my kids need homework?"

In addition to providing children with the opportunity to practise and improve academic skills, homework teaches **responsibility, self-discipline, independence, perseverance** and **time management**. These skills have a large impact on an individual's success in life.

Parenting is about teaching our children to teach themselves. By supporting them in achieving their scholastic goals and requirements, we help them to feel capable. If we value education, our children must see it in our actions in addition to our words. Here are a few tips to help parents and children make the most of doing homework.

Keep the balance

Whose homework is it? As parents we've already done many years of homework. Too much parental involvement results in a system out of balance. A parent's role is that of a facilitator, supporting and promoting the homework process but playing only a brief role. Rather than expecting perfection, allow the teacher to see where a child has difficulty. This can help the teacher know what the student still needs to learn.

Routine

Re-establish family routines, including expectations for homework. Discuss ground rules for homework and allow your children to be active participants in this discussion (example: Math first, then Reading). Involvement allows the child to feel some control over the situation. Plan a productive time when homework fits into the daily schedule. This may vary with extra-curricular commitments.

A place for homework

Establish a consistent homework location. This will support the routine. Allowing the homework to occupy centre stage in your home may result in too much parental participation. Some children work better with music in the background, others don't. Find out what works well for your child.

Supplies

Children spend a lot of time **not** doing homework while looking for a missing ruler or eraser. Create a box of supplies that are kept at the homework location so that the pursuit of the ruler does not land them in front of the television.

What you should expect

We all know that old habits are hard to break, so don't expect a quick fix. Change can be fragile, particularly in the early stages, and relapses can occur. Try not to slip back into taking more responsibility than your role should have. Talk with your child's teacher if homework is taking longer than you expect. With open communication between teacher, student and parent, everyone can gain from this process.

I'm so mad, I could scream!
Three tips to keep you calm

Within 24 hours, we heard the same story from a few different clients. That means if it's happening to you, you are not alone. When you're in a power struggle with your child, things don't feel like they can get any worse, and you panic, there are three ways it can go: flight, freeze or fight.

Flight
I've got to get out of here now! Maybe I can race upstairs and shut the door before my kid gets to my room. Even if you do make it, you're on one side of the door and he's on the other, pounding away to let him in.

Freeze
I don't know what to do, maybe nothing? Maybe cry? WHAT do I do?

Fight
If we're going down, I'm going to be louder and uglier than she will be.

None of these really work, so when a melt-down hits, what else can we do?

STOP, DROP AND ROLL...WITH LAUGHTER

Stop
Stop talking, stop yelling. Stay silent and breathe. The silence may shock your child into a change but the best part is you won't do something that you regret.

Drop

Drop to the floor and just sit. From there, you can go from being against your child to being on the same side. The script could be, *WOW – we were really yelling. We've got a problem, how can we fix it?*

Will a hug work? A few deep breaths, maybe read a book together or just look at the ceiling for a minute and then regroup and move forward. Focus on HOW do we move on from here rather than WHY are we here?

Roll...with laughter

If you can find a way to inject humour into the situation, then you are, as they say, "Laughin'!" Use a funny voice to ask *What are we doing?* or make a funny face. Breaking the tension can get everyone moving in a new direction.

Does this mean that we just let the bad behaviour go? No. What it means is that, for the time being, the behaviour is left behind and you move forward to finish whatever needs to be finished. Get yourself out the door to school or into the kitchen to make dinner. Later, when things are a bit calmer, and you have time, you can revisit the behaviour. If a consequence had already existed, you can allow your child to experience the consequence. If you need to develop a consequence, now is the time to clarify expectations, and the consequence. In addition, clarify what strategies your child can use to avoid that misbehaviour in the future. And while you are at it, an apology for your behaviour would work well here too.

Stop, drop and roll...keep those tools in your back pocket for when your temper is on fire!

What if your child is an eagle?
Finding the good in your child

A boy found an eagle's egg and he put it in the nest of a prairie chicken. The eagle hatched and thought he was a chicken. He grew up doing what prairie chickens do — scratching at the dirt for food and flying short distances with a noisy fluttering of wings. It was a dreary life. Gradually the eagle grew old and bitter.

One day he and his prairie chicken friends saw a beautiful bird soaring on the currents of air, high above the mountains. "Oh, I wish I could fly like that!" said the eagle. The chicken replied, "Don't give it another thought. That's the mighty eagle, the king of all birds — you could never be like him!" And the eagle didn't give it another thought. He went on cackling and complaining about life. He died thinking he was a prairie chicken.

My friend, you too were born an eagle. The Creator intended you to be an eagle, so don't listen to the prairie chickens!—Native American Legend

What if you really are an eagle — or just as important, what if your child is an eagle? In fact, all children have the ability to soar; for many, it may be in a completely different area of interest from the rest of the family. Just ask Gail, who has two children who play the piano beautifully when she had never played a note, or Julie, who has a daughter with a burning passion for having hockey pucks flying at her in the goal. Julie had never even picked up a hockey stick until the age of 39. We may not understand our kids' dreams, never mind excel at them, but that doesn't really matter. What really matters is that we believe in our kids.

We need to believe in our kids because, for many years, our kids actually believe that we know what we are talking about. This is important when it comes to our kids' dreams but is even more important in our daily lives. When we tell our kids (through words or actions) that we believe they will mess up, they will. When we warn them, *Don't you throw that food on the floor like you did yesterday!* we are basically telling them that we expect them to do it again.

- *Do not walk over there and hit your brother!*

- *Don't have a tantrum when we have to leave our playdate!*

- *Do not come out of your room again!*

Our words have power and we can use them for evil or for good. What if we changed the sentences above?

- *Look at you holding that food on the tray. I knew you could do it!*

- *Thanks for being gentle with your brother as you walk by.*

- *Let's practise what we are going to say and do when we leave Jackie's house this afternoon.*

- *It is your job to lie with your head on your pillow, eyes closed and wait for sleep to come to you. I'll be back as soon as I have gone to the bathroom and I bet I'll see you fast asleep because you already seem really tired.*

Our actions can also be used for good or evil. What are we really saying when we tell our kids, *I know you can put your clothes in the laundry* as we pick up socks and a T-shirt and throw them in the hamper? Actions speak louder than words and we are really showing that we don't think that they can do it otherwise we would have had them do it themselves.

Let us get back to the legend above. What if your child has a huge love of tennis but she is really pretty average? How do you show a belief in your child when you really don't believe? Here are some ways to support your eagle living in the family of prairie chickens or a prairie chicken living with eagles.

Stay in the present
Our kids may dream that they will play in the NHL or be the first astronaut on Mars. We might not want it, we might not believe it, but we can let them dream.

- *Wow, sounds like an exciting dream!*

- *This is the perfect time of your life to dream as many dreams as you can.*

- *When I was little, I wanted to be a rock star...*

Don't worry about their dreams being crushed in the future. They may well outgrow them all on their own. And find new dreams that have a chance of coming true.

Keep it real
Not every child is going to be good at everything they love – so don't tell them they are because they won't believe you anyway. Instead of giving junk praise – *Wow, that's the best picture I've ever seen! You will be in the Olympics for sure!* – use words that notice:

- *You used a lot of green and blue together – I like how they look beside each other.*

- *You were really passing to your teammates. It's nice that you are learning to work together.*

Help them to plan

Once you see that your school-aged kids really do have a love for an activity that is completely foreign to you, talk with them about how they might learn more about this task. Are there books at the library or videos online that might help? Do you know someone who knows more about this activity?

Teach a budget

As tempting as it is to sign your little Tiger Woods Wannabe up for private golf lessons and camps every week of the summer, it may not be realistic based on time, money and life. As parents, look at your time and money budgets and set some realistic boundaries. Then get your child involved to pick and choose how the money/time can be best spent to help with his vision.

Live your values

Encourage your child to practise the values you treasure while supporting beliefs. Don't only acknowledge your child's strengths, building an unrealistic sense of self around the belief that you love her only for being the best pianist in the competition. Instead, note strengths and weaknesses and point out others that are involved in her successes. Note her perseverance when she practises to get better at a certain scale. Note her kindness when she congratulates her competitors.

Whether your little ones are at extra-curricular activities or at your kitchen table, spend some time noticing your words and actions. Determine whether you are forecasting misbehaviour or the behaviour you would like to see. Encourage your kids honestly and take advantage of teaching opportunities as they come. Ultimately, whether they are eagles or prairie chickens, help them to learn that all of us have strengths and weaknesses – we use these to be part of society; relying on others for help when we need it and lending a hand when we've got one to share. Birds of all feathers can flock together.

Tantrums – Are they just for toddlers?
Responding to temper tantrums

Parents have generally come to expect/fear/dread the two-year-old tantrum. We proclaim with wariness and acceptance that our 18-month-old is already on the way to two because the fondness for the word "NO" has begun. We know that tantrums typically occur in children ages one through three who have neither the vocabulary nor the self-control to deal with the large swings in emotion prevalent at that age.

In fact, from the parenting perspective, tantrums provide an opportunity for the child to learn to self-soothe and to manage his or her behaviour.

Our reaction to the tantrums will either help to teach those lessons or teach our child to continue to tantrum well past preschool and even elementary school.

We all know the five-year-old who tears his room apart when he is angry, or the ten-year-old who screams back at mom and dad using wonderful words that we thought they weren't hearing us say. These, in effect, are tantrums – poor strategies for managing self-control when emotional upsets rear their heads. Tantrums aren't just for toddlers if they are a means to a desired end.

What can we do?

1. **Get calm and stay calm**.
   Our children learn how to react to stressful situations from us.

Through self-monitoring (deep breath, counting, leave the room) and speaking in a calm and quiet tone, we show our children the behaviour we would like to see from them.

2. **Keep the child (and other children) safe.**
   Remove breakable or harmful objects and other children from the area or remove the child.

3. **Express expectations.**
   You seem really angry, upset… you need to get your body under control. I can't understand what you want from me when you talk this way. Please come and get me when you are ready to talk so that I can understand you.

What works for one child may not work for another – here are some strategies.

1. Some children can't calm themselves and may need to be held until they stop thrashing. You may need to help them slow their breathing. Some children respond well to music.

2. Remove yourself from the child until he/she has calmed. Reinforce the calming as soon as it starts. *Wow, you got your body under control – I knew that you could do that – You were really angry.*

3. Take the child to his/her room to calm down. We need to remember that we are not doing this as punishment, but rather teaching the child to leave a situation until he/she has control.

Children under two years of age can sometimes be distracted from a tantrum with humour or another activity.

Remember: Don't give in to a tantrum because it only teaches the child that tantrums are useful forms of behaviour. If you need more ideas, give us a call.

DECEMBER

Resilience
Coping when parenting feels overwhelming

I said NO, now go to your room and leave your brother alone!

It was three o'clock and I was already shouting. This was the kind of day I dreaded and there were still hours to go before a meal — which I had to prepare and serve — and that precious moment when the kids were in bed and I could breathe. How was I going to go on? I collapsed at the kitchen table, bent my head over the dirty lunch dishes and began to cry.

We've all been there — or somewhere close to it. Parenting throws challenges at us on a constant schedule. That is why resilience must be an attainable quality for us as parents and also for our children.

Resilience is a noun that means :

- The ability to recover quickly from depression or discouragement: *Her innate resilience helped her through the witching hour.*

- Flexibility

If our goal as parents is to raise independent, responsible, resilient individuals, we need to model those characteristics and we can't do that by spending a large amount of time sobbing into soggy PB and J crusts. But where does resilience come from? How can we get it, keep it and teach it?

A lack of resilience is evident when we find ourselves yelling at our children or their slammed bedroom doors. It is overwhelmingly absent when, out of sheer exhaustion, we give in to a tantrum or bribe a child to get what we desire. It threatens us when we dread the thought of a new day starting or the kids coming home from school. It is not a nice place to be – but one that we all find ourselves in from time to time. If you have taken up residence in this place of no resilience, it is time to make a change.

The change that brings on resilience comes in two forms:

What we say to our children
What we say to ourselves

Every time we interact with our children, we have a choice: to react thoughtlessly or to thoughtfully respond. The former may already be happening – it is exhausting. The latter takes a lot more work at the outset but feels way better when all is said and done. Knowing how we will respond when things go wrong (and when things go well) can make a huge difference in the day's outcome. Using an internal script made up of respectful language to express emotions and limits will result in your children learning to handle situations appropriately and listening to you rather than tuning you out.

We call this Parenting with a Plan. It's about evaluating recurring situations that are bringing you down and reworking those scenarios so that they turn out the way you want them to. Once you know what you want it to look like, you can create respectful language to use and you can inform your kids about the new version you are creating. This enables everyone to work toward a new family habit and keeps everyone, especially you, feeling confident and capable about handling those moments that you know are coming.

To continue feeling confident, we also need to be aware of what we are telling ourselves throughout the day. We can become pretty low if our minds are filled with:

- *She doesn't respect me, that's why she ignores me.*

- *He is going to sass me for the rest of his life – I've got 14 more years of this until he leaves home!*

- *I'm the adult here and I'd better show those kids that I'm louder and stronger than they are – then they'll listen!*

- *Why am I such a bad parent?*

We can change what we are telling ourselves to boost our resilience. When the toddler says *No* for the 34th time, we can think, *Wow, this "no" stage can be tricky. It'll pass.*

When our seven-year-old says, *You are the MEANEST MOM EVER! I HATE YOU!* we can think, *She's obviously really frustrated, she probably needs a hug.*

When our teenager says, *Mom, you just don't get it – leave me alone!* we can think, *Getting mad right now won't solve anything.* When he's calm, we'll figure out how to face this. Setting ourselves up for success internally can be one of the best ways to stay resilient. If we don't take this step, we can end up spiralling downward with depressing self-talk. Our children need us to support them through their development with a calm demeanour, especially when they are anything but calm.

Once we have begun to build resilience in ourselves and to model it for our children, we can take the time to teach it in other ways as well. Our children meet with challenges daily, both externally (*Molly and Sara didn't let me play with them today*) and internally (*How come I have such an ugly face?*). We can foster self-esteem by encouraging our children and helping them to feel that they belong, that they are loved and capable.

This is more about noticing their deeds than about judging them for what they do. This can occur when negative behaviour comes our way: *I saw you hit – that behaviour is not appropriate.*

As parents we are getting more familiar with talking about a child's "bad" behaviour rather than a "bad" child. We can apply the same techniques when behaviour is more positive: *I saw you help your brother pack his bag today – that showed kindness.*

If we strive to show unconditional love for our children, their actions shouldn't impact whether we love them or believe in them. Helping a sibling doesn't make someone a better person, just as hitting a sibling doesn't make a child a worse person.

Meeting our children where they are, encouraging their participation in problem solving, and supporting them with unconditional love will foster self-esteem and resilience Figure out how to capture it for yourself and then teach those beings who rely on you. They are watching your words and your actions. Take baby steps, breathe, and together you will find resilience.

Reclaiming the holidays
Bringing back the time of love, peace and celebration

As you rush through the mall, getting trapped behind slow-walking people, you can physically feel the clock ticking – you have exactly one hour and 32 minutes until you need to pick the little ones up from the sitter's. How can you possibly get all of the shopping done, the gifts wrapped and hidden, the cookies baked and have any energy left?

The following tips can help you to slow things down and start making the holidays what you want them to be.

Take a walk down memory lane
When we think back to holidays past, it is rare that we are able to remember what gifts we received each year. More likely, we are thinking of time spent with family, special activities, wonderful foods, music and books. These are the ingredients of tradition. Talk with your co-parent and decide together which of these traditions you would like to share with your children.

Involve the children
Ask those children who are old enough to remember, what traditions they value around this season. They may be waiting for a special cookie or wanting to light the candles and sing favourite songs. Perhaps it is a snowball fight on the lawn or delivering cookies to their friends in the neighbourhood. They will love to be asked and it's a great way to determine how you will spend the holidays.

Make a plan

Once you know what you want, figure out how to make it happen. Move things up or down on the priority list. If keeping your family healthy and well-rested is a priority, decide how many nights a week you want to be home or how many parties you will attend. If the spirit of giving is on your list, find a way (and a date on the calendar) to share that with your family. Help out at a food bank, sponsor a family, or shovel snow for those on your street who cannot.

Use your priority list to help you identify what you really want to be doing this season and to help you say no graciously to things that don't fit in.

Favour routines

With visiting relatives, celebrations and excitement and school holidays, it is pretty hard to follow routines to the letter. As parents, however, it is our responsibility to keep an eye out for our children's health and well-being. If we know that dinner is served an hour later at Grandma's than at home, plan to feed the children a healthy snack at their normal dinner time to keep them going. They can still join the family at the table and eat a smaller portion once the meal is served. Having full bellies will help them to be successful at the table.

Try to keep nap times and bedtimes on track when you can. That goes for the adults in your family as well. Play time is valuable too. If your child generally takes an afternoon walk to a playground to run off excess energy, see if you can find a playground close to where you are visiting or head to a pool for a family swim. This may well become a holiday tradition.

Take time to teach

Many parents cringe when they think about their little ones sitting down at a large formal dinner. They wonder, will their children say thank you upon receiving a gift or simply tear out of the room to play. Will they share toys with their rarely-seen cousins or share fists instead? This is another place to plan.

Make sure that your expectations for your children are realistic. Meet them where they <u>are</u> (they are not born with these skills) and set them up for success. If we take the time to teach our children, we show our children that they are valued and give them the skills that they need.

Teach and practise table manners that are appropriate for their developmental level well before you ever get to the formal dinner. Pretend to exchange gifts weeks in advance to teach and model what should be said when your child is given a gift or wished Merry Christmas, Happy Chanukah or whatever the greeting may be. When we give our children vocabulary and manners, we are sharing gifts that will last a lifetime.

Family is Community One
Our kids learn what they live and live what they learn. If you believe that generosity is important in your family, start within your home. Work with the children to generate a list of things they can do to be generous (responsibilities, baking, shovelling, making cards, giving away clothing or toys). Start in the home and then let it spin out to the community.

Keep the motivation intrinsic
There is no need to post your endeavours on Facebook or tweet about how proud you are of your family and your kids. Instead, let the joy of giving be the intrinsic motivation at this peaceful time.

Managing vs. consulting
As a parent, what is my job description?

We believe the answer is that parents are both management and consultants. As with many things in life, there is not a lot of black and white in parenting. The extremes are out there on the spectrum, but they are separated by a multitude of shades of grey. The aspects of managing our children and consulting to them also sit on a spectrum. We slide our tuner (remember stereos in the "good old days?") back and forth along this line many times in our parenting lives and while it seems logical enough, it can be emotional as well.

When we start our parenting journey, we are hands-on managers. We take responsibility for the minute-to-minute health and welfare of our children. As infants, they can do very little and it can be so confusing to figure out what they really need. Some people slide the parenting tuner all the way to managing in the beginning, while others have it a few notches short, doing a bit of consulting right from the start; watching for yawns to indicate sleepiness, learning the cries and their meanings. Gradually we all begin to tap the tuner toward consulting, even though it is certainly still in the managing half of the continuum.

As the journey continues, the child grows and, as tempting as it may be to manage everything, we know that children thrive when given responsibilities so we take the time to teach and move the knob ever more toward the consulting end. It can be exhilarating to watch our little ones grow, developing independence in their tiny actions and needing us for less and less. But it can also be a bit heart-wrenching. There is a tendency for some parents to want to preserve the naiveté of childhood and the feelings of being needed and important in our children's lives.

Sometimes, it seems that our children, who have performed a task independently for months on end, are suddenly unable to manage it. As consultants, we can check in to see whether the child understands how to fix the problem, we can even work "on-site" for a couple of days to re-teach or oversee the new plan that has been put in place (a shift in routine timing, strategies for dealing with nightmares, wording for handling the first girlfriend experience).

But as our kids learn new skills, becoming a consultant can be a difficult step. It may hit hard on their first day of preschool or the move to Kindergarten or Grade One. Perhaps the first day they take the bus or walk to school independently is the moment we feel a pang of loss, a lack of being needed.

With a move through elementary school and beyond, the tuner seems like it is forever sliding back and forth. As our kids begin new tasks, we function as a manager to set boundaries, model values and take the time to teach each task. Having done so, we slide to a consulting role, checking in to see how things are progressing and whether we can be of assistance.

Tweens and teens seem to take giant leaps of independence, wanting to act like grownups and to keep up with their peers. They start to look so much older than they were and it can be scary to believe that we have no control over their attitudes, their actions and their values. In response to this fear, some parents jump in as full-time managers, grasping at the familiar job description – the person who decides it all for their child. Other parents feel helpless, like they have to let go and let the child dive, head first into an ocean of harmful adventure. They are the off-site consultant, watching and dreading but not really wanting to say much as they watch their children sink.

It is not difficult to find ourselves back in the world of black and white as our children get older – hands-on manager (doing homework, choosing clothes, choosing friends) or off-site consultant (turning a blind eye to drinking, drugs, rudeness, parties, bullying). The emotions for the parents are huge, running the gamut:

- Fear of losing importance and worth in our child's life

- Fear that our child will make terrible choices and wreck her life

- Fear that the world is changing and that we are powerless to protect our children

- Grief at the loss of control and sense of self as super parent

- Disappointment in society and what it has become

- Disappointment and guilt for not better preparing our children

Yet, this is the time when the continuum is so important for our children. As we did when they were younger, our children need our guidance and support in navigating the almost daily changes that they encounter as they move to teenage life. If they rely only on the advice of their peers (who are, by definition, at the same life-stage as our children), they will never expand their viewpoints. Physiologically and psychologically, our children need us to manage, by setting boundaries, teaching skills and modelling values through expectations. This must happen in a "working <u>with</u> the child" format.

Our children also need us to consult as they begin to use these new strategies. Rather than telling them what to do we can continue to problem-solve with them, ask them how they plan to deal with the situation, sharing our stories of past experiences and dialoguing with them to show our support and our belief that they can do it.

While your children are in your home, you are a manager and a consultant, one who may feel grief at the loss of the past, along with hope for the future and joy for the present – the only place we really ever are.

Year in review
Making a plan for the year ahead

It first hits when the kids head back to school. We clear the third turn of the track as the final four months lie ahead. Thanksgiving finds us in the home stretch with Halloween waving the white flag – only one lap remaining. Remembrance Day and Holiday festivities get us across the finish line. Each year passes faster than the previous and each time, we resolve to live the next year "in the moment" so that we don't feel so shocked the next time September comes around.

Of course, whenever the rug is, figuratively, pulled out from under our feet, we have the opportunity to, well…buy a new rug. This is one of the best parts of the end of the year. We get a chance to reflect upon the past year and create the next.

For some, there are years that really need to be forgotten. Years where we slam the door, lock it and hope never to see such a year again. We clamour for a new year, one that hasn't been damaged by natural disaster, flagrant relationship challenges or our own mistakes. We hope that this one will be different.

Often, we don't feel quite so passionately about the months behind us, but have strong hopes for those ahead. Sometimes, in dreaming about what could be, we wipe ourselves almost completely out of the picture in an effort to change every bad habit our family has ever had.

Trying to find a more tempered approach may be the key. Certainly in business, seeing where we have been enables us to set reasonable expectations and to develop attainable goals. We may even draw lines in the sand that are a step or two beyond what we believe is possible just to push ourselves forward.

In our lives as parents, there is room for this tempered approach as well. In reviewing the year, human nature will have many of us noting what didn't happen, or where we went wrong. One way to counteract this is to make a list of the things that <u>did</u> happen or what we <u>have</u> done over the past year. This may go by month or by achievements and attempts of family members.

With this awareness, we can define areas of challenge. Did certain family habits rear their heads more than others? Are temper tantrums still cluttering the mealtime table or blocking the way to the garage in the mornings? Are we saving our worst behaviour for our nearest and dearest?

These challenges are gifts. They highlight quite clearly the areas needing our attention. Often, in studying our accomplishments and shortcomings, a common thread emerges. Certain family values that we thought were a part of our family's core are lacking or at least withering. These may be the areas to target as we look to the year ahead.

When clutter is gone, cleaning a room becomes much easier. This same system also applies to parenting. If we see the tantrums or yelling as clutter, we can put parenting strategies in place to handle each situation, but we still need to do some deeper cleaning once the clutter has been cleared away.

Teaching core values is the deep-cleaning of parenting. It is only by discussing our family's position on these values (respect, cooperation, compassion, honesty, etc.), that our children can begin to discover and form their own positions. Ultimately, they may not choose the exact same list as ours. However, they will develop an understanding that actions are guided by underlying beliefs. This then enables their self-discipline — making good choices on their own when no adult is there to help.

Having reviewed your year and the values important to you, make a list of the situations you might like to change and values you wish to teach in the year ahead. Prioritize these and then, choose one or two from the middle of the pack. Tackling the hottest issues right off the bat may carry too much emotional intensity for everyone involved. Success with slightly less-weighty challenges can get everyone feeling prepared to wade deeper into the list.

When we at Parenting Power plan for the next year, or even the next few months, we try to keep things simple so that neither we nor our children feel overwhelmed with change. By focusing on one or two values, everyone in each of our families develops an understanding of how pervasive these values are in our daily lives. We develop new habits and recognize when we attempt to put a value into use.

Reviewing the year can be a very positive experience and/or a catalyst for change. Ultimately though, it is being present each day that enables learning and growth for us and for our children. Have a wonderful New Year or 365 great New Days!

Afterword from the authors

Here we are at the end of our Year of Intentional Parenting. We started the year with a goal to promote and support the physical, emotional, social and intellectual development of our children from infancy to adulthood, through the process of creating:

- Space to determine what's important to us when it comes to the development of our kids

- Time in our calendars to allow that to happen

- Systems to allow it to happen – with respect to modelling what we want our kids to learn

In some ways, the year passed quickly and in other ways January feels so long ago. Our two families have experienced many changes this past year. These experiences enabled us to really live the above process.

Our families, and likely yours too, were faced with what is really important in terms of values and development. The business of day-to-day was forced to stop so that we could take care of what was necessary. This clarity of perspective has helped us to create processes to move forward.

As with all phases of life, we know that these processes will continue to evolve as our lives proceed and our kids grow. What likely won't change is our commitment to taking the time to focus on and support our children's development (and our own).

That's the thing about intention; it isn't particularly "flash in the pan," it is more "old growth forest." So while the year is drawing to a close, we will continue to focus on intentional parenting, next year and beyond. Here are a few more ideas to use as you continue to think about this process.

In his book, *The Power of Intention*, author Wayne Dyer outlines four steps to intention. These are **"Discipline, Wisdom, Love and Surrender."** While our perspective is a bit different, the following is a way to consider these four steps as they pertain to intentional parenting.

Discipline
Teaching ourselves to make new parenting decisions rather than following what hasn't worked before – and then sticking to the new system.

Wisdom
Learning from our experiences as things work and as they fail miserably. One of our children shared his school's definition of FAIL = First Attempt In Learning. We've adopted that as a motto around here. When things don't work, it is the perfect time to seek the wisdom in the experience and to have the discipline to work toward a new process.

Love
We wouldn't be doing any of this if we didn't love our kids. Loving them inspires us to do what is right for them rather than what is easy in the moment. It drives us to live our values.

Surrender
Give in to the reality that parenting isn't always easy and that perfect parenting doesn't exist. When you aren't holding yourself to exacting standards, it is a bit easier to weather the storms. Try to remember that, when a child misbehaves, it is very rarely about us and yet, it is easy for many of us to slip into the mindset of, "If I were a better parent, this wouldn't be happening. If I was a better parent, I could make my child behave." This mindset doesn't help anyone. It isn't about us...it is about them. Surrender to the question, "What can we do to help them learn what needs to be learned?"

Lastly, we've enjoyed our time with you this year. We feel blessed to have a business through which we connect with so many interesting, caring people who have the courage to share their stories and want to learn more.

Even though parenting isn't easy, it is worth it in so many ways. Here's to many years of great learning. We've got lots in store for you!

Julie and Gail
www.parentingpower.ca
admin@parentingpower.ca
www.facebook.com/parentingpower
Twitter: @parentingpower

Books we love

For parents

10 Conversations You Need to Have with Your Children – Shmuley Boteach

The Gifts of Imperfection – Brene Brown

Just Because It's Not Wrong Doesn't Make It Right: Teaching Kids to Think and Act Ethically – Barbara Coloroso

Parenting through Crisis: Helping Kids in Times of Loss, Grief, and Change – Barbara Coloroso

The Family Virtues Guide – Linda Kavelin Popov

The Price of Privilege – Madeline Levine

Teach Your Children Well – Madeline Levine

The Blessing of a Skinned Knee – Wendy Mogel

The Blessing of a B Minus – Wendy Mogel

Raising Self-Reliant Children in a Self-Indulgent World – H. Stephen Glenn and Jane Ed.D. Nelsen

The Big Disconnect: Protecting Childhood and Family Relationships — Catherine Steiner-Adair

The Self-Esteem Trap — Polly Young-Eisendrath

For using with kids
Boys, Girls & Body Science: A First Book About Facts of Life — Meg Hickling

A Very Touching Book…for Little People and for Big People — Jan Hindman

When I Feel Angry — Cornelia Spelman

When I Feel Worried — Cornelia Spelman

When I Feel Sad — Cornelia Spelman

When I Feel Jealous — Cornelia Spelman

When I Miss You — Cornelia Spelman

Books we cited - used with permission
The Power of Intention — Wayne Dyer, 2005 Hay House, Inc., Carlsbad, CA

The Self-Esteem Trap — Polly Young-Eisendrath, 2008 Little, Brown and Company, New York, NY

Something from Nothing — Phoebe Gilman, 1992, Scholastic Inc., New York, NY

About the Authors

Julie Freedman-Smith and Gail Bell have run Parenting Power since 2002. They are regular contributors and consultants to television and radio programs on parenting. Their writing has been published in national newspapers and popular magazines such as the *Globe and Mail* and *Today's Parent*, and they blog for the *Calgary Herald* and MumRX.com. Julie and Gail live in Calgary with their husbands and children. This is their first book.

Printed in Canada